✳ *ISSUE 006* ✳

BUCKMXN JOURNAL

Portland, OR
buckmanjournal.com
Buckman Publishing, LLC

THE BUCKMXN TEAM:

editor
jerry sampson

art director
ellen robinette

operations manager
emmi greer

**buckmxn associate
& freelance poolboy**
rich perin

designer
hannah johnson

cover photos by lyudmila zotova

IN THIS ISSUE

WRITERS

KESHA AJOSE-FISHER (she/her) is an Oregon Book Award winner, an Oregon Literary Fellow and an expert at spotting bedtime manipulation. Much of her written work is guided by her childhood in Africa and America. She lives in Portland with her hilarious Kevin, their s'more-obsessed children, and two adorable poodles. She is currently working on her memoir and advocating for more kindness in the world.

STEVEN BRYAN BIELER (he/him) bats right, throws right, leans left. His stories have most recently appeared in *Across the Margin, Catapult,* and *Slow Trains.* He attended the Tin House workshop, the Clarion West workshop, and various workshops his employers claimed were for his own good. He lives in Portland, Oregon, with his wife, the mystery writer Deborah Donnelly, their dogs, and their mortgage.

CASEY CARPENTER (she/they) is a Portland-based writer originally from Texas. She writes about her body. This is her first publication.

S CEARLEY is a former AI researcher who has tricked a computer into making poetry when it thinks it is making art. He currently lives 20 cm above a river watching birds, otters, and drunk fishermen.

MAX FORSTAG writes personal narratives and creative nonfiction short stories on themes of self-discovery. A lover of maps, he was raised in Northeast Ohio and has lived in South America and West Africa. He speaks passable Spanish and enough Twi to prevent getting overcharged for a Ghanaian *tro tro* ride. Max studies creative nonfiction at *The Attic Institute.* He also writes about his favorite sport for *The Baseball Times* newsletter. When not writing, he sings other people's stories in a seven-piece cover band. Max lives in Portland with his wife and two cats. This is his first publication.

CHANEL HEART (pronoun indifferent) is a Jamaican-American writer, illustrator, and performance designer creating quiet and emotional artwork about relationships, identity, dreams, nature, magic, and hair. Heart crafted several art performances for K-5 afterschool programming with Splendorporium Art4Life. These included a one-act retelling of *The Agony and the Ecstasy* and "A Traditional Fairy Friendship Wedding" with paper flowers. Heart's writing can be found in Theories of HER: An Experimental Anthology and soon on Twitter @ fromEveryst Stories. Heart's current focus is a magical realism novella about the one worst thing in the world. Raised in York, Nebraska, Heart now lives in Portland.

JORDAN HERNANDEZ (she/her) is a Portland-based writer and former Southerner. She has been a freelance writer for over a decade, and regularly writes and contributes to various publications both in print and online. She believes in storytelling as the most tender and honest way to get to know and learn about human beings in all aspects of life. You can find her reading, exploring and traveling through different parts of Oregon and beyond, sneaking chocolate from the stash in the back of her freezer when no one is looking, or next to the cheese at any party.

FRANCES LU-PAI IPPOLITO (she/her) is an emerging Chinese American writer in Portland, Oregon. When she's not spending time with her children in the outdoors, she's busy crafting short stories in horror, sci-fi, fantasy, or whatever genre-bending she can get away with. Her stories have appeared in *Nailed Magazine*, *HauntedMTL*, and *Red Penguin Collections*. Her work has also been featured at the Ooligan Press Writers of Color Showcase 2020 in Portland, Oregon.

AVVY MAR (she/her) is a writer, trauma therapist and current fiction student in the Creative Writing MFA program at Pacific University. Her poetry has been published in *Beyond Words* literary Journal. She lives in Portland, Oregon with her family, including two teenage daughters who assure her they could write better than she can.

JENNIFER "JP" PERRINE is the award-winning author of four books of poetry: *Again*, *The Body Is No Machine*, *In the Human Zoo*, and *No Confession, No Mass*. Their recent short stories and essays appear in *The Gay & Lesbian Review*, *Valparaiso Fiction Review*, and *Literal Latte*. JP serves as a guest editor for Broadsided Press and a co-editor at Airlie Press, a consensus-based poetry collective. JP lives in Portland, Oregon, where they co-host the Incite: Queer Writers Read series and teach creative writing and intersectional equity practices to youth and adults. To learn more, visit www.jenniferperrine.org.

NATHAN WADE CARTER (he/him) is a queer, grey-a, non-binary poet, musician, and artist living in Portland, Oregon. His chapbook is ROYGBIV (Ursus Americanus Press 2017). He is the editor and founder of SUSAN / The Journal. He writes and performs songs under the name Purrbot. Find him online at nathanwadecarter.com.

KRISTIN WALROD (she/her)'s stories have appeared in *Prism Review*, *Literal Latte*, *NervyGirl*, *Stringtown*, *Storyglossia* and have been shortlisted for the *The Masters Review Volume V Anthology* and *Fish Publishing* Flash Fiction Prize 2016; and as a semi-finalist in the 2017 Raymond Carver Short Story Contest. She serves on the National Advisory Council of Graywolf Press and is an assistant editor at *Narrative Magazine*. For over two decades, she has taught creative writing in literacy programs, community colleges and K-12 schools as a writer-in-residence.

SALIMATU AMABEBE (they/he), is a Bay Area-based chef, multimedia artist and the founder/director of Black Feast. Amabebe's work focuses on the intersection of food and art, drawing from family memories, Nigerian recipes, and Black culinary history.

IG: @salimatuamabebe

DAN BOTHWELL (he/him) Dan Bothwell creates line art illustrations with ink, paper, and occasionally colored pencils. Some of his previous works have been featured in the short film *La Contessa*, and his most recent piece was donated to a silent auction for charity. His focus is on the strangeness and emotion of everyday items and scenes whether it be a candy wrapper, a cracked egg, or a wrapped present. Dan aims to illustrate surreal images in a realistic way to visually capture our intangible moods and emotions.

danbothwell.com

IG: @asolidseven

BENJAMIN CHAN (he/him) Benjamin is an analog photographer based in Portland, Oregon. He is a member of The Portland Darkroom, a member-supported community space for the practice of analog photography whose mission is to keep film photography alive and accessible in Portland.

chanalogfoto.com

IG: @chanalogfoto

email: ben@chanalogfoto.com

ISIS FISHER (she/they) works in a range of mediums playing with the juxtaposition of intricate, detailed imagery and simplified abstraction. The work explores concepts of shadow self, the strength of femininity and interconnectivity often using archetypal and mythological symbolism. It addresses how the subconscious manifestations of the individual relate to the state of humanity as a whole.

isisfisher.art

IG: @_isisfisher_

ANNIKA HANSTEEN-IZORA (she/they) is a queer Black poet, designer, and writer from Palo Alto, California, based in Brooklyn, New York. As a multimedia artist, Annika uses poetry, design, and performance to explore themes of healing, Black liberation, afrofuturism, and queerness. She is a creative contributor at Black Feast and the Creative Director of Design and UI at Ethel's Club and Somewhere Good, a to-be-released social media platform that connects people of color to each other and the things they love. Annika believes in the sacredness of Black joy, and uses her work to explore tenderness as a liberation practice.

annikaizora.com

IG: @annika.izora

SYLVIE HUHN (she/her) The topical matter of Sylvie's work ranges from climate anxiety, urban deconstruction/reconstruction vs. natural habitat in the Pacific Northwest, and archival memory. Using mixed media, she methodically builds up the surfaces of her paintings with layers including printed ephemera, found objects, and fragments of personal photo-transfers – the visual, verbal and numerical information she could never retain in memory. She paints over these cluttered systems as an attempt to embalm chaos in a skin. This use of landscape and layering continues in her other practices, such as pinhole photography, video, and sound distortion. She pursued art because the subject of information internalization has been a continuous battle with a learning disability/short-term working memory. She has embraced this battle by earning her MLS, with a concentration in archives, and now working in data/records simultaneously with her creative practices.

sylviedakotahuhn.com

IG: @sylviedakota

STS

MICHAEL LEE (he/him) is a self taught analog photographer interested in seeing and capturing what others may not.

IG: @fixedwithyou

twitter: @fixedwithyou

JEREMY LE GRAND (he/him) is an artist and fabricator living and working in Portland, OR. His work often uses patterns, iteration, and rhythm to build dense, abstract compositions based on fragments of bodies and the natural world. About his work: 'We gathered to catch a glimpse. (Of ourselves and each other). Our dumb humanity in a colorful russet potato. Eyes peeking through patterned paper, from inside another. A wash of color over a striped veil, concealing a blob of anxiety. The patterns repeat, stack and diffuse, iterate and mirror and mimic. They are not ghosts! These are wandering forms birthed from the slap of a palm on a forehead. A dumbfounded genesis. A primeval grunt.'

jeremylegrand.com

IG: @jeremythegrand

ANYA ROBERTS-TONEY (she/her) Anya Roberts-Toney's oil paintings and works on paper explore themes related to femininity and feminine power. Her work has been exhibited locally and nationally at locations including Disjecta Contemporary Art Center, Dust to Dust Projects, Nationale, The Portland 'Pataphysical Society, the Office at Russo Lee, Somos Gallery, and Stephanie Chefas Projects. She is a recipient of the Stumptown Artist Fellowship and an Oregon Arts Commission Career Opportunity Grant, with additional funding from the Ford Family Foundation. Anya received her BA in Studio Art from Brown University and her MFA in Visual Studies from Pacific Northwest College of Art. Originally from Seattle, WA, she lives and works in Portland, OR, where she is represented by Nationale.

anyarobertstoney.com

IG: @anyajrt

TENYA RODRIGUEZ (they/them) As a self taught artist, Tenya finds time at work and at home to commune with their ancestors through art. Their work is primarily made on found/recycled paper and with various types of handwriting tools.

IG: @tenyarodriguez

LARA ROUSE (she/her). Lara makes art without a clear message in mind. Time is of the essence at her house, all art is made between making meals, reading books, and trips to the park with her daughter. To her, collage is like putting puzzle pieces together -- you get a certain feeling when everything fits right.

IG: @good_luck_lara

SAMANTHA WALL (she/her), originally from Seoul, South Korea, is an artist working in Portland, Oregon. Wall immigrated to the United States as a child and comes from a multiracial background. Operating from within this framework, her drawings embody the experience of navigating transcultural identity. Her projects have been exhibited at the Hangaram Art Museum in the Seoul Arts Center, CUE Art Foundation in New York, and the Portland Art Museum, as well as exhibition spaces in New Orleans, Los Angeles, and Frankfurt. She is the recipient of numerous grants and awards including an MFA Grant from the Joan Mitchell Foundation, a Golden Spot Residency Award from Crow's Shadow Institute for the Arts, and a Hallie Ford Fellowship from the Ford Family Foundation.

samanthawall.com

IG:: @samanthawall

facebook.com/samanthawall5

A WAY BACK

written by kesha ajose-fisher
art by samantha wall

Fatai did not kiss me *goodnight* anymore. His *good-night darlings* and *I love yous* slowly waned then ceased. This shift in my life was like day folding into night—one minute the sun was caressing my neck, the next I was in the dark. Fatai worked, came home, played with our daughter, exercised in our home gym, showered, then faded into his iPhone at bed-time. He watched whatever he wanted without input from me, and he gamed with strangers, and scrolled through Instagram, laughing until his eyes were wet before tucking the phone neatly beneath his pillow. First thing in the morning, he reached for it and began another day.

The last time Fatai kissed me—goodnight or otherwise—our doctor had smiled and nodded, and I exhaled in relief that finally, our family of three was becoming four. I expected an embrace or a peck from my husband, but he raised his head to ask if I was well enough to attend a Christmas party that night. The doctor missed my somber expression. Fatai contended it would be a reason to celebrate our news. I complied.

With my hair pulled back and body squeezed into a

full-length black dress and diamond studs, I came out of my closet and languidly spun around.

"See, you don't even look pregnant."

I watched Fatai's boundless energy at the party while I explained to strangers that *yes*, some Nigerians have light skin and *yes*, I was still black. Fatai was surrounded by women who clung to his every word while I tried to find a way out of a conversation with a woman who *homegirled* me though we had never met.

"Hey sister girl?" she said. I answered with a simple hello. She went on about how much she loved Beyonce and how the singer was now her spirit animal. I nodded and smiled and took measured sips of my water through her tedious tale. When I managed an exit from that conversation, I was suddenly pulled into a new query by a man who clearly had never interacted with a person of color outside of work or solely in a domestic capacity. He wanted to know if I had seen the new Kevin Hart Special on Netflix.

"No, sorry. I haven't."

He then proceeded to share a joke about Michael Jackson and Elvis Presley walking into a bar. I pointed to the white at the tip of his nose then made my escape when he cupped his face in embarrassment. Fatai did not notice me tugging on my ear until I hunched over cradling my abdomen. He dropped his conversation then and led me outside. In the car, I said, laughing, "Thank God. These *Oyinbo* people are mad, o. I needed to get out of there."

His shoulders sagged. "So you're okay?"

"No, I'm tired."

"Come on," he groaned. "One more drink?"

Before I could respond, he had turned the car around. Three gin and tonics later, I drove us home. We swapped black-tie for pajamas and brushed our teeth side by side in silence. We climbed into bed. He gave me his back then commanded Alexa to dim the lights.

"Goodnight, Fatai. I love you."

"Good night."

"Don't you love me?"

"*Ah ahn*, of course, I love you."

"Then say it."

"Every time?"

"Yes. I need to hear it."

"I love you."

"Thank you, Fatai."

He faced me and traced my flat tummy with his finger. "I hope it's a boy."

"Me too, so I can be done."

"Done, *ke*? We're just getting started."

"The factory is closed after this one, whatever it is."

"Ah, no, o. Unless it's *omo okunrin*, we will go back to the well until you fetch me my son."

I laughed. "Cricket will be the best big sister. I can just see them both running around my father's compound, speaking Yoruba."

He nodded. "Yeah," then pressed his gin-soaked mouth to mine. "Good night, Mango."

I knew even before asking that Fatai would shut me out. He had caught that Portland malady, a condition of passive aggressivity where one ignores a problem in hopes that it dies. He had become *Portland nice*.

When I first moved to Oregon, I had not known that I would be the only black person in all areas of my life. I lived in my West side neighborhood for a year and never had one real conversation with any of my neighbors. They waved to me on my way to collecting the mail, and I quickly learned that should anyone ask how I was doing, a response beyond *fine* was not expected. 'How are you' did not mean 'how are you' like *bawo ni* and *shay Alafia ni* as it did back home. The question was merely a newfangled version of the tipping of one's hat, a courteous nod in passing. Too many times at work I heard, "Margot, you're such a good friend," but I could never call upon any of them when I was scared, or when loneliness pushed me

> **'How are you' did not mean 'how are you' like bawo ni and shay Alafia ni as it did back home. The question was merely a newfangled version of the tipping of one's hat, a courteous nod in passing.**

into a corner—not even when Papa died—so I decided to move back home. Then, Fatai called.

Fatai burst through the security gates at the airport and fell to his knees with arms stretched above his head as if tasting freedom for the first time. I worried he would kiss the floor that had been trampled on and photographed by so many it had its own hashtag: *#PDXCarpet*. I quickly aided him onto his feet, and we had a better kiss than our first—before life stepped between us. He had grown a full sharp beard and the rest of him was built as if carved from *wenge* wood and just as black. He garnered and relished in the attention I did not want, and I faded into the background where I was comfortable. He became my very own piece of Africa, and I felt at home in him, at least for a while.

Fatai loved Portland, all of Oregon, really. He was the only Nigerian I knew who hiked for enjoyment. He drank beer like water and dragged me to every spot on the *Best of Oregon* breweries list. We wed surrounded by colossal pines that seemed to be holding hands with the sky, in front of fifty friends that Fatai magically assembled at the top of Mount Tabor. He danced a hole into the floor as the guests cheered him on, and I wished only that Papa had been there, so I had someone to talk to. I told Fatai that night, that I wanted to move back to Nigeria, and he went silent. After Cricket was born, I asked again. He dove deeper into his pool of friends then, and I feared that if I continued harping on the matter, that I, we would become outsiders in his world. I let it go.

Now, eight months from the last time I attempted to revisit my request, after news of our second pregnancy, I feared a new kind of loss. Much of last night's agument had escalated due to his usual gavel drop.

"I'm still speaking," I said after he unexpectedly called on Alexa to quell the lights. He tuned in to his phone then tuned me out. I sat in the dark, hot under the collar unsure of my next move.

He said, "Goodnight, babe. I love you."

Once Fatai was done, we were done, so I turned over and replied, "I love you, too." I could have ordered the lights back on and dropped all my rage on his head, but what would that kind of explosion do to us?

There was no revisiting the matter once we slept on it. It was Fatai's greatest maneuver. Morning sprang upon us and I patted his side of the bed to find only warm sheets. I heard the thuds of the punching bag downstairs and sat up.

To my right, the sun had scattered clouds across the Portland skyline and stretched its arms through our panoramic window. Ten years with Fatai, and *look at your life*, still came to mind each day while I climbed into a silk robe that cost more than my wedding dress. I glanced at my clock and kept my ears perked for when Fatai would roar to celebrate the end of his workout. I rushed to the bathroom as swiftly as my enormous waist allowed, then I crammed my thighs into red spandex leggings and snapped on a beige tank top. The arc of my belly with its obtruded navel hung like a massive teat over my waistband. I could not tie my shoes, so I texted Sochima.

She wrote back: *Inside kitchen, mah.*

"Good morning, Madam," Sochima said, before lacing me up.

"Soon you go *dey* dress me, *ehn*?" I joked.

"If you want, mah."

My *Verve Life* energy drink glowed green atop the counter. I grabbed it. "*Shay* Cricket still *dey* sleep?" I asked Sochima.

"Yes, mah. And *Oga dey* exercising."

"I heard him."

I followed the hall off the kitchen toward the gym. Sochima's flute-heavy music

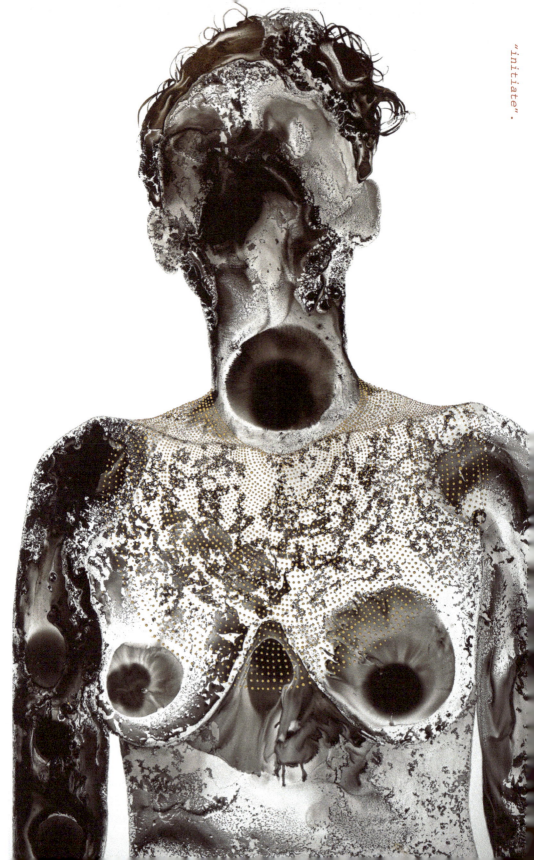

floated out the speakers and yielded to the whirring fans when I opened the door. Fatai was on the treadmill. He smiled as I climbed onto the Peloton bike that cost more than my first car. I rode, head down, surrounded by gym equipment that cost more than my first home. When I looked up, I decided, *yes*, I could set it all ablaze for a chance to live in Nigeria again.

The last time I was home, Mr. Agbe had said, "All yours," as we parked in front of Papa's compound. I sighed with tearful relief when the chain of keys landed heavily in my palm as if exhausted by their own journey.

"Madam, are you okay?" Mr. Agbe asked.

I embraced him. He nodded with a tight grin and straightened his suit. I ran giddily through the dying gardens before suddenly dropping to my knees.

Mr. Agbe stood over me. "Do you want me to stay with you?"

I glanced up at him. He must have thought me mad there on my knees weeping over the stump of a mango tree. I dragged my sleeve past my nostrils and said, "No, I'm fine." His body abruptly vanished with the compound when Fatai's roar rattled my head.

I stopped pedaling. "Fatai, why must you be so loud when you finish?"

He firmed his biceps. "A lion always roars after every conquer. Doesn't it?"

"You're no lion."

He kissed my cheek and winked. "So you say now."

I resumed my pedaling. "Babe, can we chat?"

"Now?" He glanced at his watch. "I have a meeting soon."

"Over Zoom?"

He stuttered. "I'm, err, actually going in."

I frowned. "Are you?"

"For this client, yes."

"Your client should stay home too. It's dire out there, remember?"

"You know I hate arguing before work, Margot."

I stopped pedaling when he used my given name. "Who is arguing?" I spoke sweetly. "Fifty minutes is plenty of time. I'll even drive."

Hands atop his head, his face froze confusedly as if he were stranded at a fork in the road. "Mango, *kilo ti e sele*?"

I lifted my feet off the dock. "What happened?"

"That *kekere* argument?" He shrugged. "It was nothing. We are not moving back. Full stop."

My head and voice lifted. "Don't do that."

He inched away from the bike, palms up. "Another pregnancy tantrum, is it?"

I climbed off.

"Mango," he chuckled. "You're angry, sweating for nothing. You didn't even hit your miles."

"I'm pregnant, Fatai. I'm allowed to be fat."

"Who said anything about fat?"

"*Ma* change topic. I am showering, then coming with you. Full stop."

He scratched his scalp. "How will you get home?"

I waved my phone.

He slid between the door and me. "So you will enter Lyft *pelu* pandemic—while you're pregnant with my son? Smart."

> **When I looked up, I decided, yes, I could set it all ablaze for a chance to live in Nigeria again.**

"Fine. I'll drive your car. You Lyft home."

He wagged his finger. "Margot, stop this, o."

I walked away.

Sochima was feeding Cricket in the kitchen. An odor of boiled eggs filled my nostrils.

"Open window, Sochima. Please."

"Right away, Madam," she said, moving with the measured pace of an elderly woman.

I kissed my daughter atop her head. "Sochima, plait this girl's hair. Please?"

"Yes, Madam, I go do Cricket hair fine-fine."

"Oh, from now on, we go *dey* use only her Yoruba name."

Sochima nodded then handed my daughter her sippy cup.

"Mommy's juice." I said, before pointing to hers. "Iretiola's juice."

Iretiola drew it to her chest. "Mine doose."

Sochima said, "Smarty Pant."

I stole a deep breath. After a soft exhale I said, "Sochima?"

She lowered the spoon from her mouth. "Sorry Madam. *Shay* make I don't say this?"

"No. It's okay. I want ask you. *Shay* you like America?"

"Plenty, Madam."

"And Nigeria *seff*?"

She was silent.

"You *wan* go back?"

She shook her head. "Madam. I like make I *dey* work for you and *Oga*, now."

"If I say I *wan* send you go *nko*?"

Sochima took her hands up in supplication. "No, mah. *Abeg*, no sack me, mah."

I took her hand and lowered them onto the table. "No be that. I just come *dey* wonder, which place be say like home?"

She scanned the floor as if searching for the correct answer.

"Sochima," I said, breaking her gaze with the ground. "Nigeria or America?"

She shrugged. "I no know, o."

"Talk woman to woman."

She masked her smile with her hand and water swelled in her eyes. "Madam, I pray say make I put my hand touch my son and him wife and *dem pikin*— my grand-children again." She pinched off her tears. "But, anywhere *bettah* pass nowhere, mah."

We were smiling at each other when Fatai's footsteps punctured the silence. Sochima knelt to greet him. Fatai kissed Iretiola's cheek and rose with yolk in the nest of his beard.

"How's my Cricket?" he sang.

"Fatai, speak more Yoruba to Iretiola, please."

He tipped his invisible cap. "*Ekaro*, Iretiola. *Omo ninu emi mi. Omo ife aye, ife anu.* Is that better, Mango?"

I rolled my eyes. Iretiola and Sochima chuckled. Fatai peeled off his shirt and said on his way up, "Sochima, no breakfast for me today."

I whispered to her after his exit, "I *done* buy your ticket."

She eyed her folded hands on the table. "Okay, mah. I go ring my son say I *dey* come live *wit* him."

"Sochima? No. I want make you go live for my papa compound; manage *am* before I—I mean, we come."

"Mah?"

"You go go wait for us. The compound get water for swimming, for catch fish. Trees *dey* everywhere: pawpaw, orange, banana, *agbalumo*, pear; plus— my new mango tree."

She bowed. "Yes, mah."

"I remember rainy season, *sha*. I go *dey* sit under my mango tree make rain fall for my head. Come dry season, I go swim every day, then I go sit under am from day

"anchor".

to night. That tree *done* die now. The new one small-small, but—still, you go like this my papa house."

"True talk, mah?"

I took her hand. "Please, tell me."

"I no go swim, o."

We laughed and hugged while my shoulder collected her tears.

"*Shay* make I go tell *Oga* thank you?"

My eyes swelled and my palms went up. "No!"

She flinched.

"No mention anything to *Oga*, please."

She squinted and tilted her head. I shrugged. We met in that place where women knew to find each other in solidarity. She nodded and brought her hands over mine. I eyed the weathered skin on the hands she had used to tend to Iretiola since her first breath, hands she had used to keep me grounded, hands I needed in my life regardless of where I landed.

"Listen, Madam," she said, demonstrating on herself. "*Wahala* inside head and *wahala* inside heart big, big pass any other kind *wahala*. You understand?"

I bowed.

While Sochima cleaned the sticky yolk off Iretiola's face, I wandered back to that cool Lagos evening when Papa's compound first became mine. Beyond the blood in my veins and the Yoruba on my tongue, Mr. Agbe was most helpful in my reclaiming Nigeria as home. The property had been rotting at the hands of a covetous *asewo* who alleged that Papa married her—without evidence. Mr. Agbe spent a year after my father's funeral, battling the courts on my behalf to remove her for poisoning Papa though we also had no proof. I had returned to Oregon for work. Each month, Mr. Agbe called to assure me we were getting closer, that God and the law sided with us.

I told Mr. Agbe when he gave me the keys that I would be moving back permanently, once I sold *Verve Life Juices*. I was going to tend to the decaying bungalow and regrow the tree that Papa's prostitute had razed for its connection to me. Children around Lagos would visit my property freely, roaming the forest. My own children would play there too, should I have them one day, and Mr. Agbe promised to pray on it. When I shared the news with Fatai, he had received an offer from Intel that nobody refuses, he said. We stayed.

"Madam. You okay?" Sochima asked, tapping my forearm.

"Yes, Sochima. I go tell *Oga* today."

I was sitting on our bed, jingling Fatai's keys when he came out in a suit for the first time in months.

He sighed. "Still?"

I nodded. "Your chariot awaits."

✳✳✳

Fatai raised the volume on the radio while backing out of the garage.

"Mango, remember when we saw Mos Def at the Crystal?"

"God, he kept complaining about the heat. And he half-assed *Ms. Fat booty*—all the money we spent."

"Maybe he was just uncomfortable. Think about that?"

I shrugged and grabbed the bar above my head. "Take it easy, Mr. Driver. Want me to stain your leather?"

"Sorry," he laughed. "The road moved. You know Yasiin Bey changed his name."

"Who?"

"Mos Def. His real name was Dante Smith, and he—"

While Fatai recalled our courting days, I remembered standing behind him in the security line at Murtala Muhammad airport shaking my head at his obstinance. Fatai refused to pay one *kobo*. It was commonly known that when traveling through the airport, one must bring at least five hundred naira in small change to dole out between check-in and boarding, but that Fatai, my God, he had strong head, *sha*. He removed the tongues of his pockets and shrugged with his hands up. "I don't have anything for you."

I thought him thick, though his verve moved me.

"You are lucky to be getting on this plane," I told him at our gate.

"I won't be bullied by no man, man," he said.

"Are you Yoruba?" I asked.

"I am. *Omo Eko ni mi, o.* From Obalende, proper."

He made me laugh.

"You?"

"Raised here. *Omo Eko ni mi, o.* Ikoyi proper."

I made him laugh.

"*Shay oyinbo ni e?*"

"No," I responded to the question that always followed *where are you from?* "My late mum was white—French. Papa is Yoruba, but I came out looking like sliced bread—*bi pafun.*"

He offered his hand. "The name is Fatai."

I gave him mine. "Margot."

"*Bi* mango?"

I pulled back. "Funny. Papa calls me Mango because as a kid, I would sit under our mango tree for hours just daydreaming."

"Mango it is."

He ordered four meatpies and two cokes. I offered to pay. He pushed back my purse. We started chatting.

"I am going to New York, you?"

"Oregon."

"Ore-what?"

"On the west coast," I said. "Between California and Washington. Sorry, the other Washington."

"Now I am confused."

I laughed. "So was I. I'm starting an energy drink company. You?"

"I'm an engineer," he began, then he roamed in and out of my head for nearly two hours until the loud-speaker's warbled announcements called us aboard. He even switched his first-class seat for a spot next to me. In London, we devoured a nine-hour stop like crisps. At baggage claim in New York, I offered my hand. "It was nice to meet you Fatai."

He shook my hand and gazed at me with eyes so deep and black, I got lost in them. I suppose that was why he presumed I wanted a kiss.

"Is that okay?"

"No," I replied. Then I moved in for a better one.

He held on to my hand. "I'm under contract for three years," he said. "Will you wait for me?"

"How about we promise no such thing. If we meet again, we make it forever?"

"If that's a proposal, I accept," he said, then he roared as he left me.

Three years later, he moved to Oregon and took a loathsome sales job. We found an apartment in Lake Oswego because Fatai enjoyed the appearance of success. "LO has the best schools," he had said. I acquiesced though we had no children. Fatai drove a Lexus that garnered attention because he believed it eased white people's minds about their black neighbor. He showed me off because of how black he was and how white he knew they all thought I was. No day passed without him attempting to prove himself worthy of them, their time, their laughter, their friendship, and it always broke my heart.

Soon, we became *oko* and *iyawo*. Intel called. We hired Sochima from Lagos to help with Iretiola, then we moved into a house atop a hill overlooking a city at war with police on a nightly basis. Things had fallen apart in March across America after a police officer sealed a black man's fate with a knee to his neck. People around the world poured into the streets over all the blood shed by black bodies. Even Portland became an epicenter for the Black Lives Matter movement, white as it was. Although I was elated to see my neighbors standing up, I dreaded the fallout. I watched in despair as police gassed protestors and our friends split over differing positions while the president egged it on. Weeks into those protests, I learned I was having a son.

My knees buckled inside the elevator outside our doctor's office. I glared at Fatai. "I will not raise a son in this country."

He avoided the topic then. He avoided it throughout the pregnancy, and he was avoiding it again as he recalled our past. I was due in weeks, and *I* faced a fork in the road: an ultimatum or complacency. I tightened my grip on the bar above my head and blurted out, "We are moving back to Nigeria."

He swerved suddenly out of his lane and parked on the shoulder of the highway. After killing the engine, he yelled. "Be my peace!"

"I am."

"No," he shouted again, as loudly as I had ever heard it. "That is all I ever ask." His tone cooled. "Be the peace I need to keep hustling for your red bottoms, your Pelotons and panoramic views. You know what I got? No life and no friends, because you want me right in your pocket like a sweet saved for later."

"I never did that."

"But you shunned my friends and called them racist when they were only joking with you."

'So America is without problems as we roll a Tesla along the highway flanked by people living in tents? Concealing misery does not make it disappear, Fatai. At least in Nigeria, you know what you're getting with friends and the way people treat their neighbors.'

"Racism is not funny, Fatai."

"You're so much like them, you don't even know. Fighting against a system that you've only benefitted from; look at your life—your whiteness too. All you do is paint a rosy picture of a place rife with abject poverty by romanticizing your father's decrepit compound because it's in Af-ree-kah."

My eyes moistened and my voice cracked. "That's unfair."

"I pulled it from thin air then?"

"So America is without problems as we roll a Tesla along the highway flanked by people living in tents? Concealing misery does not make it disappear, Fatai. At least in Nigeria, you know what you're getting with friends and the way people treat their neighbors."

"Are my sacrifices not enough?"

"I sacrificed too, Fatai. I stayed here for you. I struggled too."

"Struggled?"

"Fatai, I grew up with a single father—don't scoff—in a small house with nothing."

"*O pa mi lerin*—I laugh. A paradise with just you and *daddy* was nothing? Seven of us lived in a box. I sold kerosene to eat. You get me? That is having nothing, not this, your distorted version of suffering because your mum wasn't there to iron out the wrinkles in your life."

"Fatai, I don't want to fight. I just want you, and to protect our children. Can't you see? We are being hunted and gutted without repercussions. Who said it: *the eye of this boil is red and soft and ready to erupt?* Well, I aim to be far from the gore when it does."

"We stayed when Cricket was born."

"We stayed because you ignored my requests."

"No. You used that request as leverage to control me."

"How?"

"You gave me an ultimatum, saying you were lonely here; so I stopped hanging out with my friends."

"I won't rehash that nonsense. Plus, it's different with

> *I raised my hands to my ears and kept my eyes on the dashboard. My heart commenced its frenzied dance, the one I loathed profoundly because it arrived solely in the presence of police.*

a son. You cannot know my burden."

He pointed to the back of his hand. "Margot, I live it every day."

"You're only emphasizing my point."

His shoulders slumped. "I've taken care of you. Have I not? Why *baje*?"

"Who's choosing vanity over sanity now?"

He frowned. "You're spoiling everything."

I slowed the moment with a deep breath. "Listen, a while back, I was trying to parallel park, and this white guy was getting annoyed with me. I waved at him, feeling bad. He rolled down his window and said, 'Stupid Nigger.' I walked into my book club looking flustered, and the women—all white—asked what happened. I told them the man had said, 'Stupid idiot' instead."

"Why?"

"Because how are you does not really mean how are you."

"So, you shake off imperfect people like Harry and Meghan shook the Royals—no, no, don't laugh—then you're disingenuous with the friends you do have?"

"Don't joke. It's all so exhausting."

"Nigerian police are no different—I know you have seen that news."

"The devil I know, Fatai."

"What if I said I'm not going, Margot. What then?"

I cast my eyes on the drops of rain atop his Tesla and spoke tearfully, "We would go without you."

"You would take my children?"

"No. I would save your children."

He slapped the steering wheel. "I'm not going!"

I steadied my breaths. "Fine. Stay."

He zipped back into traffic. Sirens flashed behind us. He slapped the steering wheel repeatedly.

"Take it easy, Fatai."

He took calming breaths then cracked open the window and his glistening veneers.

"Fatai, put on your mask."

He spread on the charm in a British-tilting accent, "Good day, sir."

My hand shook atop his knee. I noticed in my side mirror a second officer resting his hand near his gun.

"Hands where I can see *em'*," he ordered.

I raised my hands to my ears and kept my eyes on the dashboard. My heart commenced its frenzied dance, the one I loathed profoundly because it arrived solely in the presence of police.

Fatai narrated his actions:

"I'm reaching for my wallet.

Pulling it out.

My license, registration, and insurance.

Anything else?"

"Is this your vehicle?"

I answered, "Our insurance states it."

Fatai faced the man with hands still on the wheel. "It *is*—sir."

"Sir?" I spoke stiffly. "*Oga e ni?*"

They both glared at me.

"Problem, madam?"

"Yes," I said, tapping my watch. "You're delaying us."

"Feisty one, there."

Fatai nodded. "She's pregnant and—"

"Fatai. Don't do that."

The officer laughed. "Watch how you slide into traffic next time— sir."

My husband was nodding and bowing as if his spine liquefied. After the officer pulled away, my heart sank, and tears poured out of me. Fatai ripped off his mask and sighed as if relieved.

I said, "*Ina e ti ku*," then awaited his wrath.

"You used to find me stubborn," he chuckled. "Now I'm weak?"

I took his hand up to my cheek. "*Ma binu*, my love."

He wiped my tears. More composed, he spoke, "Where would we even begin in Nigeria?"

"*Ah ahn*. With nothing, we built a mountain *ninu* America, right?"

He straightened his collar. "We did, didn't we?"

I winked.

"Starting from scratch is not easy, o?"

"Who are you telling?"

He kissed me. "Okay, Mango. You win."

I gazed into the black of his eyes and said, "I know. I won't be bullied by no man, man." ✳

GILLY

written by jennifer perrine
art by michael lee

On the island, I never went to school, though there was a schoolhouse attached to the old nondenominational church. Neither got any use anymore, unless by *use* you count Gilly and me sneaking into the church at night. The church, with its little ramshackle classroom tucked through a door behind the pulpit, was the only abandoned building on the island.

Gilly and I would come to the church to hear our voices echo against the empty room, the vaulted ceiling. We discovered the echo purely by accident while scavenging the church, looking for treasures. There weren't any—either there never were or someone else swept through long ago and carried them off—but that echo was more precious. On the island, our voices never bounced back: not off the sea, not off the stretch of houses that ran the length of the only road, not off the fields and beaches that stretched between buildings and boundless salt-water. In the church, we could imagine—we could *hear*—the voices of other kids our age. We knew they existed if only we listened, if only we shouted back.

On the night that Gilly and I had chosen to make good on our pact to run away together, Gilly brought

"v two".

to the church her craft scissors, a flashlight, and the Polaroid camera her grand-mother sent last Christmas. She took a single photo as a memento of what she called my *girl hair* before she began cutting, the flashlight wedged between her teeth.

She'd only just finished, just begun to gather together all the pale hair pooled on the wood floor, when we heard other voices, low talk coming from the school-house. After our first visit to the church, Gilly and I never went in the classroom—it didn't echo the way the church did, and it was too dark, windowless. When we heard people in there, Gilly was afraid we'd get caught, wanted to leave before someone saw us, but I didn't want to look like a chicken, not ever, but especially not in front of Gilly.

I tiptoed to the door that separated us from the schoolhouse and bent my ear to it, but still I couldn't make out more than muttering. Whatever was happening behind that door, listening in wasn't going to help. I gave Gilly a shrug, and we picked our way quietly back across the church, out the door, and into the night.

"Let's go," Gilly said, tugging at the hem of my shirt. I pulled away, leaving her standing in the moonlight, and walked through the waist-high weeds to the back of the church. The schoolhouse's one exterior door, which had been locked tight for as long as I could remember, now stood open a crack. Something flicked past the door, and I sank down into the weeds. I could hear Gilly rustling through the field somewhere to my left, and I wanted to motion to her, to tell her to get down, but I didn't want to be seen. I didn't want to be seen with Gilly.

Everyone on the island must have known about us. No one ever said as much, but they had other ways of letting us know. Gilly's mom told her she was spending too much time with me, suggested that Gilly go to school on the mainland where she could make other friends. Mrs. Tanner had even gone so far as to talk to Mr. Whitby, who took his boat to the mainland most days to restock the general store and pick up and drop off our post, about the possibility of ferrying Gilly back and forth to school. Gilly had begged off, promising that she'd try the mainland school next year, that she'd stay away from me, but she still snuck out most nights to meet me at the church.

My own mother knew that I was counting down the years until I turned eighteen and could move off the island, so she wasn't about to suggest shipping me off to a mainland school. She was so much subtler than Mrs. Tanner—in fact, Mama never once suggested I spend less time with Gilly, never tried to separate us. No, Mama went right to the source: she knew what I was doing with Gilly wasn't about situation or circumstance. It was about *me*. So she tried to change me, transform me into someone else.

Mama was a hippie who, when she found out she was pregnant with me, moved to the island to run away from a world that demanded she settle down, content among the endless rows of cookie-cutter houses, beneath plumes that billowed from her hometown power plant. She came here to commune with the seas and the sky. When Gilly and I got close, Mama tried to remake me in her image, sewing me the same flowing skirts and flowery blouses she wore. I hadn't grown much in the last year, but even so, my jeans were uncomfortably tight around my hips, my t-shirts pinched at my underarms. I gave in and started wearing the new clothes Mama had made, but when I snuck out at night to meet Gilly, I always changed first. Gilly was worth a little discomfort.

I knew if Gilly and I got caught snooping around the church, Mrs. Tanner wouldn't hold off until next year. Gilly would start school on the mainland as soon as summer ended. She'd make new friends, start dating, fall in love, and move away forever. I wanted to know who was in the schoolhouse, but not as much as I wanted to keep what Gilly and I had away from prying eyes. I crawled through the field, meeting her a few yards away, and reached up to grab her hand. I pulled her down next to me and held her, nodding to the schoolhouse and holding a finger to her lips, hoping she'd keep silent.

"We just need to wait until they're gone," I whispered.

"If we leave now—" Gilly said, too loudly.

"If we leave now, they might see us. Better to wait." Maybe we could get away without being seen, but I knew we needed a failsafe. Whoever was in the schoolhouse, they were sneaking around in the middle of the night, just like Gilly and me. Chances were, they had a secret, too, and if they knew we'd seen them, they weren't likely to go blabbing to our

> *Everyone on the island must have known about us. No one ever said as much, but they had other ways of letting us know.*

mothers and risk revealing their own late-night activities.

I watched the schoolhouse door, Gilly trembling beside me, her hand flitting toward mine, then away. I couldn't bear her nervousness and finally grabbed her hand in both of mine and squeezed gently. I tried to think of something soothing to say, but Gilly's free hand rose up and tangled in what was left of my hair, and I knew she was trying to comfort me, too. I looked at her, all black hair and pale skin in the moonlight, and leaned in to kiss her, but the achy squeal of the schoolhouse door interrupted us, turned us into tense, taut wires again.

Two figures stumbled out into the field, one heavyset and one much smaller. At first, I didn't recognize either of them, but their voices carried in the still night air.

"I have to get back," the small one said, and Gilly gasped, one short, sharp breath. I tugged at her hand, trying to keep her still, but she was already on her feet, shaking me off.

"Mom?" she asked, so quietly at first that I hoped no one had heard her. "Mom?"

"Gilly! What are you—" Mrs. Tanner backed up, hit the side of the schoolhouse, and looked around frantically. When she emerged from under the eaves again, she strode forward with more determination. "Gilly, I was worried about you! What are you doing out here in the middle of the night? Mr. Whitby and I have been looking for you for hours." Her voice came out squeaky, strung tight, and I could hear her moving through the field, the tall grass *shush*ing as she parted it.

Gilly reached down and squeezed my hand once, quickly, before bolting across the field, back toward the main road. Mrs. Tanner started after her, but Mr. Whitby grabbed her arm. "Wait," he said. "What are you going to tell her?" Mrs. Tanner pulled away from him. "Please, David. I need to talk to her."

Gilly's mother had never been the impetuous sort. She was no hippie, hadn't moved to the island to escape the evils of the world. No, Maryann Tanner had come to the island as a retreat from grief. When her husband died, she'd moved out of the home they'd lived in for seven years and plunked herself down with little toddler Gilly on Manta Island. She'd never given any thought to moving back to the mainland—or if she had, she never mentioned it to Gilly—and all of us on the island expected her to live out her days in mourning for Mr. Tanner, taken so young.

Where my mother taught me to forage mushrooms and harvest nettles and tell which berries were safe to eat straight from the vine, Mrs. Tanner had given Gilly a proper education, shipping in books and even a piano so Gilly might know all the things a girl ought to. I knew the name of every plant on this island, every insect that landed on my hand or crawled across my foot, but Gilly always knew more. She read every newspaper, every magazine, anything she could get from the mainland, and she studied the people and places in them as if they were exotic flora and fauna—which, I suppose, they were.

Which is how Gilly got the idea to cut my hair. She knew my mother would never do it. "Hair," Mama liked to say, "should be natural, too." No razors in our house, and she'd always kept my hair long and wild. "Tame hair means you're a tame woman," she'd say, picking out whatever leaf or bit of pollen snagged in the nest atop my head.

Gilly loved my hair, called it the treasure hoard. She was always running her fingers through it, pretending it was a stream of coins slipping through, shimmering. So I was surprised when she made a plan to cut it off. "It'll be easier for us that way," she said. "With your hair short, everyone will think you're a boy."

I wanted to be offended, but I knew it was true. Gilly in her crisp white shirts with the Peter Pan collars, her hair strewn with ribbons or barrettes or baubles that highlighted her fair skin, her lanky, thin-boned body. Me, short and lean in my jeans and T-shirts or button-downs gleaned from mainland thrift stores. And my face, as I can see it now in the photo Gilly took on that night: sweet, charming, but not a bit girlish. Looking at that photo, I see the wiry muscles in my forearms and calves, even in the flex of my jaw, and my first thought is *I could have been a baseball player*. If baseball players could name every flower they encountered, if they tossed off their uniforms for hand-me-downs that made them look two generations older than they actually were.

I wasn't bitter about living on the island, or looking like a boy. In some ways, it was better there than it might have been anywhere else. On the island, Gilly and I might have been scrutinized, but we never had hallways packed with other kids jeering us, never

'Tame hair means you're a tame woman,' she'd say, picking out whatever leaf or bit of pollen snagged in the nest atop my head.

"green garden".

had fights after school. Our little town might have felt confining at times, but the island was a harbor. It had always been a safe place, even for girls like us.

That was, until Ronny moved to the island. Ronny was only a few years older than us, but he'd had some trouble that no one would get specific about, at least not in front of Gilly or me. We only knew he'd dropped out of high school, come to the island to live with his uncle, Mr. Whitby, to get away from whatever bad influences had been plaguing him. "Cleaning up and making a new start" was how Mrs. Whitby described it to my mother on the day Ronny moved in. "Everyone deserves a second chance."

My mother was skeptical, eyed Ronny's crew cut and easy grin and told me to stay away from him. "Who knows what he's been up to?" she said, wiping her hands on her skirt.

It was easy enough for her to tell me to stay away, but the island was a small place, and it was only so long before Ronny started showing up wherever Gilly was. It had been hard for me to get time alone with her before, but then Ronny started dropping by her house in the morning, walking with her to the beach, where they plucked pebbles from the sand and chucked them back at the sea. I know because I spied on them, pretending I was only taking a walk nearby or looking for a good spot to fish. I'd see them sitting, talking—about what, I couldn't hear—and a flare would rise up in my cheeks, two blooms of bull thistle against the sand of my skin.

Gilly would tell me at night, at the church, that I had nothing to worry about, nothing to be jealous of, that he just needed a friend, but even she changed her tune the day that Ronny tried to kiss her, called her a tease when she pulled away, grabbed at her shirt with his thick hands and tried to drag her back to him. After that, Gilly stayed at home, leaving only at night to see me, but I knew even that was a risk. What if Ronny saw us heading to the church? What if he followed us there?

We made our plan to escape, to cut my hair, to steal the cash Mrs. Tanner had hidden in her bedside drawer, to take Mr. Whitby's boat and leave in the night, make our way as best we could in the wide world we'd only seen in Gilly's magazines, only read about in Gilly's books.

After Mrs. Tanner and Mr. Whitby left, I stood up among the weeds, trying to figure out where Gilly might have gone. I needed to see her, make sure she was okay, but I couldn't let Mrs. Tanner see me. I headed toward Gilly's house, spotting Mrs. Tanner up ahead of me. I slowed, keeping my distance, and watched as lights came on in the house, listened as Mrs. Tanner called out Gilly's name. I sat among the fiddlehead ferns that bordered their yard and waited for Gilly to answer back, but only saw Mrs. Tanner running back through the front door, back out to the road. "Gilly?" she called, hurrying down the dark path, but still, the night remained silent.

Once Mrs. Tanner was out of sight, I cut back through the woods, headed for the beach. Gilly wasn't in her usual spot, so I picked my way south, back toward the road that divided the island, and that's when I heard her: Gilly, screaming, her voice unmistakable, painful, a bad note through a flute. I raced across the sand, feeling it slip into my shoes and grate against my heels, rubbing my skin raw. The air felt thick, as if it were pushing back against me, but I kept moving, following the sound of Gilly's voice.

It was coming from the Whitbys' house, perched on its stilts along the boundary where sand met stone. I ran up the steps carved in the rock and saw him—Ronny, groping at Gilly while she screamed and screamed.

"Get off of her," I wailed, lunging for him, but he lifted his arm, smacking me away. I scrambled back to my feet and came at him again, throwing my fist hard at his face. I'd never hit anyone before, and there was a sickening crunch as my hand connected with his nose. My hand stung, full of nettles, and I bit back tears, trying to get to Gilly, to grab her and get her away.

It wasn't until I had her in my arms, rocking and comforting her, that I saw the blood, a black blot spread over the white of her shirt. I turned back to Ronny, furious, but couldn't spot him in the dim light from the Whitbys' house. "Gilly, it's going to be okay," I said. "Let's get you somewhere safe—"

"She killed him," Gilly said, rising to her feet. She swayed there, and I stood, too, grabbing her waist to keep her from falling.

"Gilly, you'll be all right. Let's get you inside the house, and I'll ask Mrs. Whitby to—"

Gilly shoved at me, screeching. "No!" She turned away, running back toward the road, but stumbled and fell, cursing. I'd never heard Gilly curse before.

I tried to help her up, but she shrugged me off, her hands covering her face. Her breath hitched and she barely got out the words again. "She— She killed him." She pulled one hand from her face, waving it back at the Whitbys' house. I knew then what she meant, though I couldn't believe it was true. I hesitated, not wanting to leave Gilly alone out there, but I didn't know what else to do. I went inside.

Mr. Whitby was on the floor in the entryway, and even in the dim light I could see his head was misshapen, a piece of it dented in. His glasses had been knocked from his face, and without them, he looked sterner, tougher, not the squat, mole-like man who brought our post and traded us his finds from the mainland for vegetables from our garden. I wanted to be sad that he was dead, but the truth was, even though he was only one of thirty-four people on the island, I never knew him very well. I was more abhorred by the starkness of his body, so clearly dead, like the baby mice I'd sometimes find in the winter, after we'd set out the poison, their tiny round eyes startled, their mouths ever so slightly open.

I couldn't look at Mr. Whitby any longer. I glanced back at Gilly, still puddled on the ground outside, before stepping over Mr. Whitby's body and making my way into the living room. Ronny was there, holding his aunt, and when I came in, I expected him to run at me, chase me off for hitting him, but he didn't. He just stared at me, glaring, cold.

"Why?" I said. It was the only question that seemed to matter, the only thing I couldn't understand. Mrs. Whitby, though, just stared off into the corner, as if I'd never spoken.

Ronny spat a glob of blood onto the floor, where it glistened against the dark wood. "Go ask your girlfriend why." He tucked his aunt's head close to his chest, smoothing her hair, shushing her, even though she wasn't making a sound.

After the night Mr. Whitby died, my mother forbade me from seeing Gilly, nailed my bedroom window shut so I couldn't sneak out at night, but it wouldn't have mattered anyway. Gilly wanted nothing to do with me. The couple of times we crossed paths by chance, she turned red, started crying, ran off as quickly as she could.

Gilly and her mother moved to the mainland later that summer, packed up their belongings and chartered a ferry to bring them across to the shore. On the day they left, I went back to the church, found the photo Gilly had taken, still nested there in a pile of my hair. I ran my thumb over the picture's slick surface, remembering Gilly's fingers tracing my scalp, the snick of her scissors at the nape of my neck. I called out Gilly's name, letting the echo bring her back to me again and again, fainter each time, until even that trace of her disappeared. *

flash fiction by casey carpenter

art by jeremy le grand

CHEERLEADER BREAST CAMP

There is a photograph. You will laugh when you see it. It is of maybe thirteen or fourteen newly adolescent girls. It is cheerleading camp. The group is all lined up in their fitted grey t-shirts, two rows of them standing on bleachers and smiling at the camera. One girl has her chest sticking out, her padded bra like "Hurray! This, This!" All the others are standing normal, like their chests exist structurally, but not as the defining feature, not the thing random people touch or name or put their face to.

It is funny. The photo is funny. I was that girl in the padded bra. When I see it, I do that thing where you laugh and then you start to cry and then you laugh and cry at the same time and cannot stop and then you try to laugh harder to cover the cry but the cry begins to rumble and swell and your laugh gets more urgent and panicked and then there is a sound coming out of you that is not a laugh or a cry, but a kind of howl, like you are some kind of animal, looking for something to speak to.

"beanie baby".

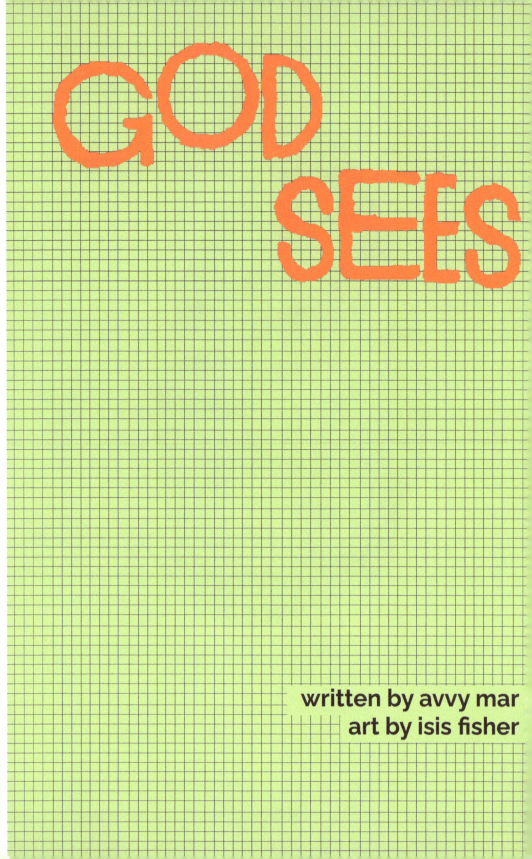

GOD SEES

written by avvy mar
art by isis fisher

`The only non-Jew I knew at Maimonides Elementary was Mrs. Wallace. She answered all the school's phone calls and typed letters at her desk outside the principal's office. She knew where to find every school supply in the huge dark hallway closet, and which kid was where in the building, even at recess. Rabbi Shimansky called her, "the glue that keeps this *meshugana* place running smoothly." The other ladies who worked at school, rabbis' wives who taught afternoons when we were allowed to speak English, kept their heads covered with scarves or wigs. Mrs. Wallace wore her white hair permed tight like a little cap that matched her pearl necklace. During the thickest cold of the winter of 1970, Mrs. Wallace had to listen to two separate bomb threats. After each, she pulled down the slender red bar on the fire alarm, the callers informing her all the Jew kids were about to burn.

Our second-grade classroom was the farthest one from the school office, so the alarm was hard to hear when kids got rowdy. But things were pretty quiet in the mornings when Rabbi Hyman taught us Hebrew and Bible stories. He only ever called on boys when we all raised our hands, so us girls mostly practiced writing Hebrew letters. The Rabbi's voice rose when he taught one of the jealous God tales, but the clang of the alarm and the murmur of other children shuffling into the hallway came right through into the silent room. We looked up from our heavy books and waited for directions.

The first bomb threat arrived in January. Maimonides School didn't have an evacuation plan. The teachers herded all the kids in a jumble into the hall just as the school day started, then whooshed us out into the starless black of a daylight savings time morning. One of the school buses hadn't left yet, so all five grades crammed four-to-a-seat at the far end of the parking lot, Mrs. Wallace the last one to leave. After she'd made sure all the schoolrooms were empty, she took a head count on the bus, and then waited alone in her white Buick with the dome light on inside. We were happy postponing Bible study, and cheered when the firetrucks, trumpeting their sirens, rushed up the hill. Firemen and policemen talked into radios in white puffs of air, while our teachers made us sing in Hebrew. A couple of the boys had a Spiderman comic they passed around. Judy Lepson found some red yarn in her coat pocket and we played Cat's Cradle. After an hour, the police said we were safe to return and left. Mrs. Wallace waved us back in from the front door.

> **The Rabbi's voice rose when he taught one of the jealous God tales, but the clang of the alarm and the murmur of other children shuffling into the hallway came right through into the silent room.**

That morning, our Bible lesson was modesty. The heroine of the Old Testament story, a teenage Jewish girl in ancient Israel, was sentenced to death because of her faith, each of her limbs tied to a different horse. A whip cracked and four horses took flight in different directions. Just before her execution, the girl drove sewing pins through her dress into her legs, fastening her skin to the cloth. The Rabbi praised the girl's courage, so devout that she'd perished protecting her purity. I kept thinking of the horses. Horses swished their gentle tails at flies. Horses had dark, liquidy eyes that made girls whisper secrets into their soft, long faces. Horses didn't hate anyone.

The second bomb threat happened one month later. In the afternoons, my class transformed into giggly English-speakers. We only half-listened to poor Mrs. Horshander. That day, Mrs. Wallace appeared in the doorway in her long blue coat. We were wound up, just back from recess. Judy and I twitched with victory; we'd finally reached ninety each in our jump rope contest. My legs felt noodly. Plus, Mrs. Horshander had surprised us with glossy new math workbooks while we were still breathing hard and fidgeting. Fresh, chemical-scented workbooks only arrived in September, so the uncracked spines and bits of newsprint clinging to the edges had us giddy. I kept sliding my hand over the chilly purple cover. Mrs. Wallace frowned at Mrs. Horshander and said, "Sharon."

Mrs. Horshander crossed the room to her, tugging at her black wig. Her fake curls slid around her head like a hat, and inched down her forehead during the day. She hooked her index finger into the gap between the wig and her shaved head, and tucked the thing behind her ear like a hood, switching from one side to the other.

While she whispered with Mrs. Horshander, Mrs. Wallace glanced down at the four tables of kids as if watching us from far, far away. Like Mom looked sometimes, gloomy and distant, while she watched Walter Cronkite in the evening, Dad already half-asleep in his living room La-Z-Boy. Sitting at the kitchen table, cigarette in hand after she'd wiped down the counters and started the dishwasher, Mom would squint at the television from a room away. That winter she shook her head at the news in Northern Ireland, school buses on fire and soldiers with their faces hidden behind ski masks. Maybe Mrs. Wallace looked at us all sad and dreamy because she was safe. No one hated Christian ladies like her.

Mrs. Horshander raised her voice and said we had to leave. When she commanded "Hurry! Hurry!" in Hebrew, the word sounded like *My Hair! My Hair!* and as she said it, she yanked her wig. We cracked up, but didn't budge. She frowned, then repeated the order louder in English. Teachers never said *bomb threat* to us; only our parents told us, and only after we were safe at home at night.

I was tracing the edges of my new math workbook. Mrs. Horshander shouted again that we had to leave. Mrs. Wallace clapped her hands. Then I threw up. My stomach didn't even hurt. One minute I was caressing my workbook, the next minute water filled my mouth. A wet slap of vomit fell and spread like honey across my shiny book. Next to me, Judy yelped and started crying. By bedtime, I'd have a raging fever, but that afternoon I rose from my seat, confused. More vomit spilled out of me onto the table. Mrs. Horshander flapped her hands at me. Heat swept down my arms. Robbie Rosenblatt, who was far away from me anyway, put his hand over his mouth like he might throw up but behind his palm he was faking, and all smiles. My teacher moved behind me, turned my shoulders away from the table toward the bathroom in the rear of the classroom. She gave me a gentle push.

Inside the bathroom, the alarm echoed loud. I made it as far as the row of sinks before the next wave of acidy liquid came up. My hands wobbled on the edges of the porcelain. A swirl of whispers and jackets being zipped, then it was quiet. I wanted my mom. Pressed against the cool sink, the muscles in my stomach cramped. Tap water washed the brownish liquid down. I lifted my head. Mrs. Wallace stood in the doorway behind me, her face unreadable in the mirror. The grandma voice I was used to vanished.

"Not the sink!" she yelled at me. "You throw up in the toilet, don't you know that?"

I didn't understand. My hands hung straight down. Hiccupping sobs burst out of me.

She pointed to the toilet stall.

"You. Dirty. Thing." She said, her neck erupting in red blotches under her tiny pearls, her necklace hanging like a circle of baby teeth.

My throat burned. I couldn't do one right thing. Liquid rushed up again. Spitting it out, I coughed so hard I peed my pants. Mrs. Wallace pointed again, her other hand wrapped around the knob of the bathroom door.

She tapped her ring against the edge of the door. A blue stone and a pearl glowed side by side like unmatched eyes. I moved to the toilet and spat out what was left.

I'd never been afraid of Mrs. Wallace, now I wanted her to disappear. The retching slowed, then stopped and the crying drained out of me. When I stood back up and flushed, I smelled hairspray, the scent of my parent's bedroom whenever Mom and Dad dressed up for dinner parties. But Mrs. Wallace didn't look like

"fire spirit".

Mom did on those nights she clouded the air with Aquanet, and drew Cleopatra lines around her eyes.

Heat spread inside my chest. My lungs burned, and a voice in my head told me why Mrs. Wallace wouldn't look at me.

"Wash your face, we need to go," she said to the floor.

The cold water I slapped on my face splashed down my dress.

I bet Mrs. Wallace thought when I left the bathroom that I'd put on my coat and snow boots. Instead, I kicked off my saddle shoes and crossed the room to my cubby on the opposite wall. My mom had put a giant Ziploc labeled *Frieda Extra Clothes* in the red bin at the bottom of the open compartment labeled *Nassauer*. With my back turned, I shimmied my tights and underwear off under my dress and pulled on the stretchy red pants from the bag. My damp dress came next. Finally, I tugged my sweatshirt on over my sweaty undershirt. Mrs. Wallace huffed behind me. The sweatshirt was from last year and felt too tight under my arms. The inside of my thighs were sticky and itchy with pee. Outside the classroom window, snow flew sideways in the grey afternoon. Once my boots were on, everything touching my skin made me more mad. I glared at Mrs. Wallace with hard eyes and tried to make my voice mean, the way my dad growled at Kyle McGreevey's grandpa when he called me and my friend Janey "the kike and the darkie" at last summer's block party.

"Go to hell," I said.

Mrs. Wallace's eyebrows shot up, but she just grabbed my hand and led me into the hall without turning the lights out. The alarm wailed in the empty corridor. Her fingers were bony, but she didn't squeeze too hard. The double doors at the end of the hall stood open to the parking lot and snow blowing in had already melted into a widening puddle. The soft wool of her coat sleeve against my wrist, Mrs. Wallace looked like Mrs. Wallace again.

We were halfway out when she let go of my hand and said, "Go on ahead."

I trudged into the crowd of my classmates in the empty parking lot. When I turned back to the doors of the school, Mrs. Wallace was gone. Snow swept in curtains across my eyelashes. Jonathon Steiner tapped my sleeve. I shrugged, then shrugged again, over and over. The two adults shook their heads, their faces more worried than last time. I jumped up and down. Kids besides me did too, but just from the cold. My face turned to the snow and sky, I jumped harder and harder until my feet hurt inside my boots. Jonathon pointed at tire tracks leaving the school. I stopped, the cold sinking in with a shudder that cleared the last of the heat in my chest. Jonathon said "Bus, too full." The rest of the school had left us behind.

Our mob of eight-year-olds, Mrs. Horshander and our principal stood in the wind. Headlights of grimy cars crept through the slush on Monroe Avenue.

The Rabbi pointed across the street to the row of identical sad-faced houses with single garage doors under them. We managed a solid straight line march to the corner, excited by the danger. The boys held onto their Yarmulkes, their heads frosted by clumps of falling snow. The sausage curls of their hair-sprayed pais bounced over their ears.

We all glanced back at the giant brick cube of Temple Beth Shalom, its brightly lit row of classrooms stretching into the parking lot while we waited to cross the street. Sirens bleated from far away. The stained-glass wall of the synagogue glowed from inside.

I put my head down and walked in Jonathon's footsteps once the light changed. Drivers' faces concentrated on the road. They peered out their windshields, grown-ups who'd never been asked where their horns were, or why their parents killed Jesus. My neighbor Janey and I had taught each other all the bad words we learned that some kids yelled at Black kids and Jewish kids. Our moms once caught us saying *Heeb! Heeb! Heeb!*, and in return got our mouths washed out with soap.

> **They peered out their windshields, grownups who'd never been asked where their horns were, or why their parents killed Jesus.**

Once we crossed the street, Rabbi Shimansky pointed at the second house, red-brown as a scab. Lights shone from the upstairs windows. He held onto the railing like a mountain climber, holding his black hat on with the other hand. All the kids squeezed in around Mrs. Horshander in the driveway. She patted some heads. I pushed the back of my hand across my mouth and spat bits of gunk on the ground.

No one opened the door. The next house was green. An old lady holding a wiener dog answered the door. My teeth felt furry. The lady tilted her head to the side as the Rabbi talked into the half-opened door. She leaned past him and squinted at our class bumping into each other in her driveway. She seemed disappointed, like the mailman only brought bills and no packages, but she nodded. We tried to stand still and look like nice kids, breathing into our mittens. Mrs. Horshander waved us up the stairs. The Rabbi hurried back across the street. I went last and got to see a police car and two firetrucks, one with a ladder, crest the hill and turn onto Monroe Avenue.

The house smelled like baby powder and the Lipton tea my mom drank. White fancy lace cloth covered the arms of the pink velvety couch. I stepped across already-slushy beach towels on the floor leading toward the kitchen. Mrs. Horshander patted my back and pointed to the wood door on the right. The lightbulb hanging over the stairs to the garage didn't shine much light. Kids crowded into the space around the wood-paneled station wagon so me and the last of my classmates sat on the steps. Mrs. Horshander closed the door behind her. Some boys made ghost sounds. Mrs. Horshander said the Rabbi had gone to meet the police and Mrs. Wallace. Two girls giggled. I peeked over the railing to see why. Rena and Leah clutched the lady's wiener dog

to their chests, other kids petting his orangey head. They named him David Cassidy.

"He's so cute." They said the same thing over and over. Me and Jonathon played Ro-Sham-Bo on the stairs even though it was boring. I was thirsty. No one acted scared, but I knew trouble awaited me. Robbie Rosenblatt made barfing sounds, but no one laughed. Mrs. Horshander leaned against the door and sighed. I knew how to hold my pee in by pressing down between my legs with my arm, so I was ok even though we were there a pretty long time.

"Frieda, are you ok?" Mrs. Horshander pressed the back of her hand against my cheek just before the lady opened her door. "Don't stand up yet. Let the other children go first."

When we stepped back into the lady's upstairs hall, my eyes stung from the light. I watched kids thank the stooped old woman standing in her kitchen doorway. She held her dog in the crook of her elbow like a purse.

"Thanks," I said, and reached out to pat David Cassidy's muzzle.

The woman jerked her dog away. "That's enough," she said, her lips gone all tight and puckery.

"You're squeezing him too hard," I said. My head thumped with the fever taking hold. The dog wanted to get down, paddling his feet in the air.

I pushed her grimy towel away with my toe. My boots traced a grey line across her pale carpeting. My teacher waited on the top step. A police car rolled out of the school's now-empty lot. Red lights spun on top of a silent ambulance. Mrs. Wallace, she fell and broke her hip, they explained a day later, but all we knew is that she never came back to school.

I grew half an inch and one whole shoe size over the next six months. Mrs. Shimansky, the principal's wife, took over answering the school phone. The third bomb threat came in April. Whatever the man whispered to Mrs. Shimansky made that the last day she was willing to work at school. Mrs. Wallace died in June, complications from her broken hip, and in July, Maimonides Elementary burned down. No bomb, just gasoline and rags and determination. No one took credit, and not a single lead or arrest. The neighbors called the firemen in time to save the temple.

Half my class didn't return that Fall, so our grade all fit in the basement pre-school downstairs from the synagogue.

The night before the memorial assembly for Mrs. Wallace that September, my mom stayed smoking more and more cigarettes at the kitchen table long after the news went off the air. The governor of New York crushed the prison riot at Attica. Dad turned off the TV, sat back down in his La-Z-Boy and stared at the black screen.

"Thirty-four people dead, " my mom said, smoke floating around her head. "Human beings wanting common decency."

I asked her why she was crying.

"Because monsters like Rockefeller run the world."

My dad called to her from his chair, "That's enough, Lenore."

She spread her hands out on the table, eyes cast down, that same faraway Mrs. Wallace gaze that made me want to run away.

All the lights in synagogue were turned on for the special assembly even though what was left of our school would have fit in four rows. From our folded chairs along the back wall, (girls and ladies weren't allowed in the cushioned pews of the temple), the ceiling seemed a mile away from the floor. The sun lit the stained glass so the pews all glowed blue and green. I pressed my shoulder blades into the metal curve of the chair I wanted to disappear into. The boys craned their necks and made faces at us, their skin sickly pale, as if they'd drowned. Rabbi Shimansky bent to the microphone on the pulpit.

"Mrs. Wallace, blessed be God, died this past summer, but breaking her hip that day is what killed her."

Sweat trickled down behind my knees. I learned the word terrorist.

"Mrs. Wallace was courageous," he said. "She saved us from someone who wanted to murder Jewish children at two o'clock." He smiled. "She emptied the whole school by 1:30."

Girls around me who'd never even talked to Mrs. Wallace wept like TV widows, hammed it up good. The crying spread like a virus. Kindergarteners started blubbering too.

"God sees all," the Rabbi reminded us. "Remember, children. God sees your sinful and virtuous actions."

My throat closed around my sinful action. I couldn't swallow. My mouth tasted like dirty pennies. I never told my Mom that Mrs. Wallace had frightened me or how gentle she was when she'd slid her long fingers out of my sweaty hand and urged me to safety while she stayed behind to corral any stray children left in the school.

"Let go, Frieda," Mrs. Horshander whispered when I wrapped my arms around her wide calves, "Get up off the floor." Her breath smelled yeasty on my cheek.

"Maybe go wash your face. " She patted my back.

I tightened my grip.

"Only our prayers help Mrs. Wallace, not this." The Rabbi was singing now, the call of his prayers murmured back by male voices. "You're all right."

"Frieda, shush, enough with you're sorry." She sighed and stopped tugging my arm.

Dark lace-up shoes moved into view beside Mrs. Horshander's scuffed flat boots. Gruff commands flew above me, orders to my teacher. She stroked my hair. Snotty tears caught in the corner of my mouth. A cloud of whimpers and sniffles surrounded me, the other girls gathering closer, drowning out the grownups' battle above us. ✳

poem by nathan wade carter

art by lara rouse

OLD GRATEFUL
AFTER EMILY KENDAL FREY

"invisible house".

how have I unclammed

forgot the beauty of other people

's accents

needed old heroes again

fed myself saltines & laughed

cried watching a superhero movie

oiled the tin man of my soul

protected the time I need for myself

what I lack

infinite

I am

as well

composted my self loathing

unnumbered my days

shared what makes me happy

felt hope

remembered old talents & passions

used my time wisely

but did not shame myself

when I needed to do nothing but plug in

pleased waiting

I cannot go faster just because it is summer

the structure of love is too well built

to be so easily demolished

let my moss grow

didn't leave the conflict

accepted compliments graciously

old grateful

gas giant

planned ahead without fear

set aside scarcity mindset

at the tapping of birds' beaks on windows

I cannot hide this kindness anymore

was saved by beautifully messy shirts

you are an improbable prophet

I am not good at parties

but sometimes I am

bloomed late

still blooming

FEAST:

LOVE LETTERS

A creation of Black narrative, an offering to Black lineage, Black Feast is a culinary event celebrating Black artists and writers through food.

Founded and directed by Salimatu Amabebe, Black Feast was created as a way to not only make space at the table for Black artists, but to design ourselves a whole new table.

At our table, guests participate in an experience that weaves together food and art. Chef Salimatu works with featured artists to create four-course, plant-based meals that act as a culinary interpretation of the artist's work. Black Feast events have featured artists across disciplines and we have had the honor of working with: Jamila Woods, Madison McFerrin, Jayy Dodd, Lukaza Branfman-Verissimo, Amenta Abioto, and many others.

With creative support from Annika Hansteen-Izora, Jasmine Beach, and Ariel Myles Hernandez, Black Feast is led by Black artists who believe in food and art as a site of possibility. Our events are a place where food celebrates Black art, Black stories, Black love, Black movement, & Black voices.

We are based in Portland, Oregon, East Bay, California, and Brooklyn, NY. All are welcome to Black Feast experiences.

This meal is created as a celebration, a dance, and an offering.

This meal is created for you.

Previous page: portrait by
Lyudmila Zotova. This page:
photo by Salimatu Amabebe.

Salimatu Amabebe (they/he), is a Bay Area-based chef, multimedia artist and the founder/director of Black Feast. Amabebe's work focuses on the intersection of food and art, drawing from family memories, Nigerian recipes, and Black culinary history.

@salimatuamabebe

Portraits by
Lyudmila Zotova,
chalice photo by
Salimatu Amabebe.

Annika Hansteen-Izora (she/they) is a queer Black poet, designer, and writer from Palo Alto, California, based in Brooklyn, New York. As a multimedia artist, Annika uses poetry, design, and performance to explore themes of healing, Black liberation, afrofuturism, and queerness.

She is a creative contributor at Black Feast and the Creative Director of Design and UI at Ethel's Club and Somewhere Good, a to-be-released social media platform that connects people of color to each other and the things they love. Annika believes in the sacredness of Black joy, and uses her work to explore tenderness as a liberation practice.

annikaizora.com

@annika.izora

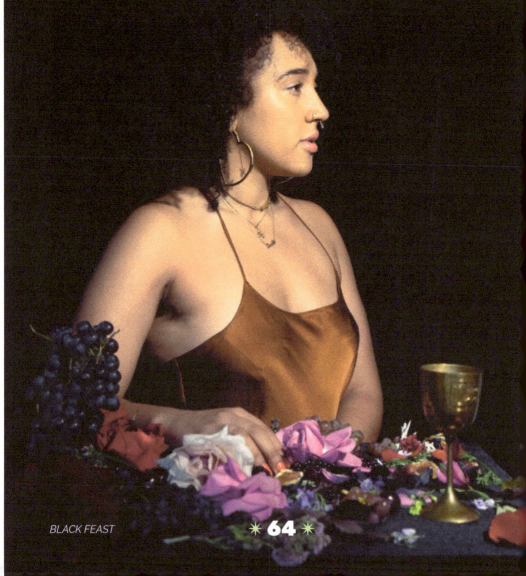

Jasmine Beach (she/her), is a multidisciplinary artist, skilled tradesperson and autonomous organizer. She is currently studying environmental policy and constitutional law with aspirations around advocating for environmental equity, mutual aid, sustainability, and decolonization.

Portraits by Lyudmila Zotova.

Ariel Myles Hernandez (they/she), is a Black and Xicanx queer person raised in the PNW. Their interior and exterior landscapes inspire them to dabble in spaces of creativity expressed through food, visual art, poetry, music, and community organizing.

After completing degrees in Black Studies and Chicano Studies, Myles Hernandez now focuses on creative and educational programming, project coordination for Black youth, art curation, and working as a core contributor to Black Feast.

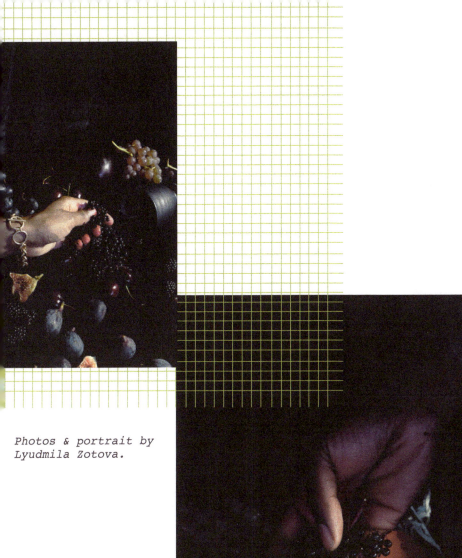

Photos & portrait by
Lyudmila Zotova.

LOVE LETTERS

was created out of insistence on Black people's right to pleasure, care, and rest. When the uprisings of 2020 began, I called Salimatu Amabebe - Founder of *Black Feast*. The first thing I asked him was: *Can I order you dinner?* I could hear Salimatu gently smile through the phone. "Yes," he responded, "Can I also order some for *you*?" That's best friends for you, still managing to take care of each other even though we're both now thousands of miles apart. I suppose, that's love for you, too, continuing to show up no matter the distance.

Salimatu and I ran *Love Letters* for 6 weeks between Portland, OR and Berkeley, CA. The premise was simple: create care packages made with items dedicated to pleasure and rest, pair it with both a love letter I'd written and a plant-based, gluten-free dessert Salimatu prepared, and give them away to any member of the Black community who wanted them for free. The meaning was deeper: we need spaces where we can hold expressions of love and compassion for ourselves and each other. We deeply need them in this age of the pandemic where many of us have been isolated from one another — where disconnection from each other is a state of emergency.

I've heard the pandemic referred to in many ways - such as an apocalypse, a dismantling. The description that has spoken to me most was author Arundhati Roy, who named the pandemic as a portal, "...a gateway between one world and the next. We can choose to walk through it, dragging the carcasses of our prejudice and hatred...Or we can walk through lightly, with little luggage, ready to imagine another world. And ready to fight for it."

The future I am ready to fight for is one where care is held at the center. And I have questions about care. I wonder what care looks like for people whose ancestors have faced transhistorical trauma. I wonder if we can get deeper on how desirability plays into care. I want to name what community and safety specifically look like, and how to move there. I have so much hope that there is a future where restorative care can be nurtured and held, both personally and interpersonally. And as Mariame Kaba named, "Hope is a discipline." Which means that it shows up in our practices, in our interpersonal relationships, in the way we hold our own bodies and hearts.

Black Feast was founded in 2016 by Salimatu as a space to center and celebrate Black people. We created *Black Feast: Love Letters* in the uprisings of 2020, an action where our joy is a site of resistance. Resistance means the refusal to accept or comply with something. When we say joy is a site of resistance, we mean that Black joy is a means of refusing to comply with the myths that white supremacy seeks to pervade — it is defiance against the idea that whiteness is supreme and those outside of it are undeserving of love, care, freedom, or life. Our joy is a site of resistance in a society which upholds the fallacy that any act outside of economic productivity is frivolous. We see rest, joy, and pleasure as instrumental aspects of healing — and so freedom and liberation. We see how new worlds can be built out of compassion, patience, and openness with one another. There is a long, long road ahead. But I deeply believe in our capacity to hold love for ourselves and each other. New worlds can begin from small acts. Like love letters. And meals prepared by someone who made it with love. In taking care of each other, we find room to design new systems, create new terms, build our own tables.

to by Lyudmila Zotova.

Photo by Lyudmila Zotova.

LOVE LETTERS

Love letter to my niggas. Love letter to my homies. Love letter to the hug where my hoop gets caught in your braid. Love letter to the group chat. To the memes and recipes and offerings to bring meals and tea. Love letter to the gass up, to our hips dancing in the light of my living room, to the way you say my name with a grinning and unapologetic mouth. Our love is a walloping melody of resistance. Our love be pulling new futures into the present. I gotchu and you got me and look at these gardens we are growing. Our care for one another is a seed from which liberation blooms. Love letter to Black women. Lover letter to Black trans folks. Love letter to Black nonbinary folks. Love letter to Black queer folks. Love letter to Black femmes. Love letter to Black children. Love letter to Black disabled folks. Love letter to Black elders. Love letter to Black men. Love letter to Black immigrants. Love letter to Black parents. Love letter to my Black loved ones. Love letter to the thunderclap of your cackle. My love, may we hold each other's hearts. May we listen to the beat. A new world is coming. This is the rhythm played before its arrival.

poem by annika hansteen-izora

photo by lyudmila zotova

BLOOM

— poem by annika hansteen-izora —

— photo by salimatu amabebe —

You are a source through which liberation blooms. You carry it in your joy, in your smile, in the dance of your hands. Praise the small thunder you carry in the way you say your name - with all the fight and liberation of the people that came before you.

Should they try and drown out your voice, you burn brighter. Should they try and make a wilt out of your name, bloom towards the sun.

On the weary days - do not forget the armies of your ancestors that prayed for your arrival.
Believe this - you are everything that your ancestors have dreamed of.
With every act of care towards yourself, you honor the folks that came before you. With every act of self love, you are creating a future where care is rooted in freedom.
We are making new worlds from our care for each other. Our communal care is a source of power. Our gentleness towards our heart is a source of strength.
This Black joy is sacred.

& I wish you joy.
I wish you rest.
I wish you the company of those you hold most dear.
I wish you love.
I wish you love.
I wish you love.

BLACK CONVENIENCE

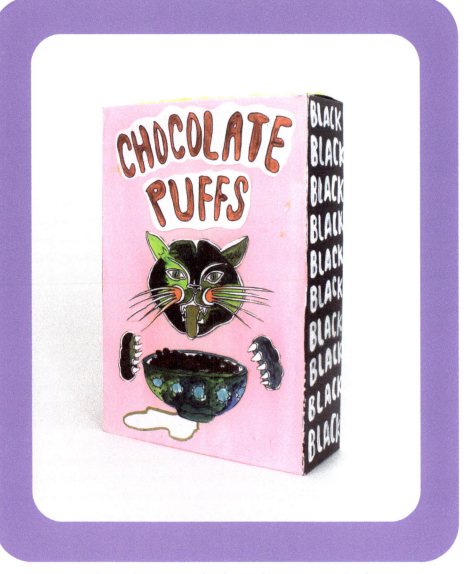

work & photography by salimatu amabebe

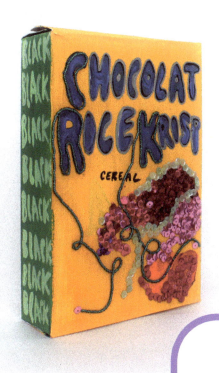

WHEN I WAS EIGHTEEN, THE SUMMER AFTER MY FIRST GIRLFRIEND BROKE UP WITH ME, I WOULD EAT ONE PANCAKE EACH DAY. MY UNCLE MADE A BIG BATCH OF CORNMEAL MOLASSES PANCAKES EVERY SUNDAY THAT WOULD LAST THROUGHOUT THE WEEK. I WANTED TO BE SMALLER BUT I DIDN'T WANT HIM TO THINK I HAD STOPPED LOVING HIS PANCAKES.

BLACK BLACK BLACK BLACK BLACK BLACK BLACK BLACK

The box reads:

Brown Sugar Cookies — Sweet!

I HAD NOT THOUGHT TOO MUCH ABOUT IT. I HADN'T THOUGHT ABOUT HOW THEY STAKED OUT OUR HOUSE, HIDING IN THE BUSHES SO THEY COULD CATCH HIM BREAKING THE RESTRAINING ORDER. I HADN'T THOUGHT ABOUT WHY THEY CHASED HIM THROUGH OUR HOUSE, DOWN THE BASEMENT STEPS WE'D JUST PAINT-ED, OUT OF THE SMALL WINDOW ——— THEIR FOOTSTEPS MARKED OUR HOME UNTIL WE HOUR?

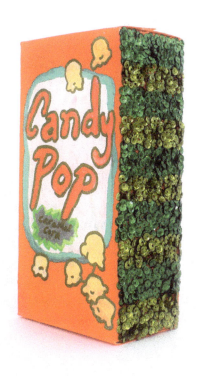

AS A CHILD, I WANTED HAIR THAT REACHED MY TOES. I THOUGHT ONE DAY I WOULD HAVE LONG, FLOWING HAIR THAT REACHED MY FEET. EVERY MONTH I WOULD CRY AS MY MOM RIPPED THE PICK FROM ROOT TO END. MY HAIR WAS PAIN. MY HAIR WAS SOMETHING I FOUGHT. I NOW COMB MY HAIR WITH PATIENCE & CARE.

WITHOUT OUR HELMETS

written by chanel heart
art by dan bothwell

In my oldest memory I am four years old sitting on the other side of a wall or curled up underneath the small kitchen table, overhearing. My mom is saying to someone on the phone, "Her brain could have been like mashed potatoes . . ." about me. She says, "That child is a miracle, vertebrate soft like an over-ripe banana and she's still alive after spending an entire day running around the house and banging into table legs!" She gasped, laughed. "I'm amazed she's even breathing some days, let alone walking, speaking..."

My brain could have been like mashed potatoes. *I* was a miracle with vertebrate soft like an over-ripe banana. She was amazed *I* was even breathing some days, walking, speaking. About me. My mother was referring to the way my head wouldn't stay up by itself.

She'd never been a poor caretaker; she did everything she should have from the moment I was born. She'd supported my head when walking me around the house, turned it purposefully to the side when I went to sleep, sat me up only after placing me in a car seat or a baby chair with a sturdy neck rest attached. I don't know what else she'd done for me as a newborn, but it had been everything right.

Most of my time from ages two to five was spent

watching TV sideways, being propped up to sip ice cream through a straw, and looking at picture books that hung from ropes tied above me like parts of a baby mobile. Every three hours I would have to turn off the TV and put my books away to listen to audio files created to send subliminal messages to my body, telling it to get stronger. But the thing is, I think I was being lied to. Not about the power of subliminal sounds, but about the whole thing.

I'm not sure if it was my mother who was lying to me or if this lie was a hand-me-down from the doctors who had lied to her about me. When I was older she would describe my condition to me by comparing other kids' heads to helium balloons and mine to a deflated balloon tied to a piece of string on a windy day. Their heads were held up by their necks, their spinal columns, and their muscles, meanwhile my head would flop down one way or the other unless I was running or being pulled by the hand quickly. If this were the case, my head would be pulled straight backwards by the law of gravity like the balloon on a string. It was around the time of this description that I began to wonder, did anyone believe this? Did it even sound possible? Had anyone ever tested to see if my head would do that or had they always settled on keeping me propped up, or laid down, or in a wheel chair with a huge neck and headrest?

But I had to admit that *I* had certainly never tried to do something I was told I wouldn't be able to do. Trying to hold my head up was something that had never crossed my mind the same way most other kids never attempted flying with their arms as wings or tried to sprout leaves from their nostrils. They'd always been told those were things they weren't capable of, so why waste good time on fruitlessness?

Since my condition had previously been unheard of, helping me learn to live with it fascinated doc-

> *Every three hours I would ... listen to audio files created to send subliminal messages to my body, telling it to get stronger. But the thing is, I think I was being lied to. Not about the power of subliminal sounds, but about the whole thing.*

tors. After I turned six the government awarded me my first skull braces. *Skull braces* were invented for me, and they worked the way that a set of hands clasped behind my head and neck would, holding me face forward. Like the braces people wear on their teeth, skull braces were meant to act as a temporary support system while my body learned to do what it was naturally meant to over time. My straight black hair was shaved down to the skull so that the intricate web of customized wires and connecters had something to cling onto when they were wrapped around my ears. Everything locked into place down my spine and behind my head. Together, these cords created a harness that miraculously restrained my head from flopping forwards or backwards ragdoll-style while I participated in everyday activities.

"Not going to be face-planting into your cereal bowls anymore now, are you?" one of the brace designers had teased. But that was something that never happened to me before so I hadn't known how to respond.

Finally I'd said, "My head is staying up." And it was.

After the braces I was directed to a specialist who created elaborate ceiling lamp covers for a living. If I was going to attend regular school I would need to keep my braces away from curious fingers and household germs, and this craftsman was going to design the protective covering I needed to do just that. It would be constructed from lightweight Plexiglass and was essentially a jar with a head-sized hole at its base as well as dozens of micro-holes throughout the remainder so that I could breathe when I had it on airtight. Just for me he'd frosted the glass light pink, and then we tried it on to make sure it wasn't too heavy.

When my mother saw the bulb around my head for the first time she started tearing up, my large dark eyes peering into hers through a thin layer of pink glass. It was a miracle.

It's a good thing I'm not claustrophobic because after that the pink globe became a part of my wardrobe, or even more so, it became a part of my body. The jar rested on my shoulders, which, over time, made me very strong in the torso. I looked like an astronaut when I wore it or like an example of what could happen to someone who got their head stuck in a fishbowl during a dare. Now equipped with braces, a pink helmet, and a somewhat grown-out buzz cut, my head was put into a classroom for the first time along with the rest of me. My mom insisted that the braces would be as different to other children as a hearing aid.

I wasn't teased in school as much as I was interrogated. Immature kids wondered why I got to wear costumes to class every day. Others were curious about what would happen if my braces disconnected. Would my head slide off of my body and bounce around on the floor like a ball? Would I still be able to talk and listen to lessons? Did I even have a regular skull in there, and if I didn't where was my brain?

Someone teased me. They were supposed to be a funny kid, and they did an impression of what might happen if my helmet broke, leaning forwards and then backwards like a dizzy person.

'Under the hood, you're like an under-cooked hard-boiled egg, you can't rush a hard-boiled egg.' So I stayed how I was.

"Isn't that how it would be?" they asked with a lighthearted smirk.

"No . . ." I shook my head slowly by the glory of my braces. "You leaned your whole body back and forth," I corrected. "It's just my head that's like that. My body's fine." But kids don't hear little details; they go for the big picture. They don't always see the familiar parts first as they've been trained to find what's different: me.

When I turned fifteen the glass was supposed to start staying at home, the braces were meant to come off, my body should now be strong and used to the weight of my head. This hypothesis was based on many studies about totally different situations from mine nine years before when the braces had first been designed. It was going to be like another part of puberty, I get a bra and I get to grow my hair out. However, I was still too soft—that's what my doctor told me—she said, "Under the hood, you're like an undercooked hard-boiled egg, you can't rush a hard-boiled egg." So I stayed how I was.

Everyone was used to me by then. I had friends, a small group of girls who made me friendship bracelets and danced with me at school parties and played on my tennis team where I had a killer backhand. I'd cycled through a couple different irregular enemies, mean girls who didn't like the way I dressed myself and some boys who stuck gum to my glass. I had a white kitten; I had a learner's permit.

The year I didn't get my braces removed a new boy transferred into our school. His name was Lukke, and his personality was both quiet and hilarious. Lukke had been a talent in boys' choir at his previous school, and he could hold a real conversation. But the best thing about him was the peculiar way he looked. It was almost as if he was inflamed, every part of him, every time of day. It wasn't like a little rosacea in the cheeks, a nose ruby from sinus issues. His skin was consistently flushed, pink as bubblegum when he was emotional.

Kids teased Lukke for real: his condition wasn't sensitive or deadly. "Little Pig!" They'd oink as he walked by and everything! Or it would be "Bubblegum Boy!"

And he was so reactive, making the bullies crazy with satisfaction. Sometimes Lukke would stop in the middle of the hallway and scream at them until his throat went raw. Other times, he'd move to a corner—to a wall barren aside from student senate campaign posters—and he'd just sit down and cry.

I was attracted to him in spite of all of this, and especially because of all of this, the pinkness and the tears. When he cried, crystal teardrops tiptoed down his pink cheeks, pink nose, pink lips, pink pointed chin. I thought that if anyone would take the time to really look at him—really admire his features individually or even all together—they would find him as handsome as I did. Past the painfully ruddy complexion, Lukke had beautiful, wide, deep-set brown eyes like dark chocolate and wonderful, soft lips, red and plump like he'd had a cherry popsicle for breakfast and then another for lunch and probably also a third for dinner. His hair was thick and naturally coiled into perfect brown ringlets around his ears and over his forehead, and his nose and cheeks were delicately peppered with strawberry freckles. He even dressed well in neat navy blue jeans that fit his long, slim legs just right and oversized cotton sweaters with the sleeves rolled up and clean sneakers.

There was something truly distinctive about him and about me that made us belong to one another. Lukke wasn't only pink in the skin, but he was really fragile. Maybe he was a hemophiliac and his parents couldn't handle it. Maybe he was a hypochondriac and even the idea of fresh air caused him to go into a sweaty panic, making him constantly red-faced like that. All I knew was that under the hood he was also an under-boiled egg, cracking under the stress.

On Halloween someone threw a party and my bracelet friends wanted to dress up Goth. We all wore as much makeup as we were allowed and chose different Gothic characters to play. I was bald Wednesday Addams. I was bald everybody. Last year I had been bald Wendy from *Peter Pan* and the year before that, a generic but bald fairy princess with flowers stapled to my dress. Lukke walked into the party with a plastic helmet around his head, and for a split-second I thought he was dressed up as me. But then I noticed the rainbow circles drawn on the outside of the glass and realized he was a gumball machine. Hilarious.

I led Lukke by the hand to the kitchen where the parents had laid out a variety of themed snacks and Halloween candies. I picked out a really nice ghost cookie and handed it to him as a peace offering. I meant to look up at him shyly when I did this, but I'd forgotten how much makeup I was wearing so I don't know if I looked shy or just scary.

"I bet you didn't think this was the way I was going to apologize." I looked into his glittering eyes. I had said something mean a few days ago for no reason.

He looked away from me quickly, blushing bright red. "I didn't think that you'd apologize at all."

His skin simply glowed. He was holding the cookie in one hand, not sure how to eat it without dismantling his Halloween costume. He looked at me with his startlingly large brown eyes.

"Do you want to kiss me?" I cooed.

The bubblegum boy stared at bald Wednesday Addams through plastic, through glass for a long time. And then he bit his lip, dimpling his cheeks and nodded. "Yes."

Before I could plan for another thing, Lukke was leaning towards me. He struggled, but worked to tilt his head correctly with the costume bulb over his head. (Who's to say it wouldn't work?) His eyes were squeezed closed in commitment and his long black eyelashes smashed down over his cheeks like bristles of a broom made to remove pink freckles.

I ducked away, "What are you doing?"

Lukke's eyes fluttered open, startled. "I thought you wanted me to kiss you..." he swallowed hard. "I—I thought you meant right now."

"untitled".

"I do mean right now," I licked my full, but chapped lips. "But without our helmets, of course."

His head moved backwards with sudden understanding. He lifted his jar from his shoulders setting it on the counter with the other Halloween treats. He waited patiently thinking, *your turn,* but out loud he asked, "Will you be okay without yours?"

I moved my head up, down, up, down, pulling at the wires at the nape of my skull, a safe, strong nod. "Yes..." The glass was to keep little kids from touching me, the germs they carry, their curiosity. But there were only costumed monsters, no little kids. "I'm fine."

I had left out the part about the worst that could happen if my braces were damaged or even if they fell off. My head, it might tip backwards and it might take me down with it. My skull might crack against the side of the kitchen counter as I fell, hurting me. Or my skull might bounce back like a rubber ball. And yet, nothing might happen. I didn't know.

Lukke and I stared at one another, the potential outcomes drifting around our heads, thickening the air and making it difficult to breathe. How much longer would I wait to take a deep inhale? And then, as if he could tell I was drowning, Lukke cupped my fishbowl head in his soft pink hands and lifted it from my shoulders, drenching me in outside air.

The sounds and smells of the party poured over me in torrents. The music was so much louder without the barrier between the speakers and my ears. The kitchen now smelled sickeningly sweet from all the sugary snacks and handmade treats made with confectioner's flour and dyes in weird colors like black, orange, and purple, like anyone wanted to eat a cupcake that tasted like purple. The colors of our costumes looked bolder without the thin sheet of glass literally tinting the world rose, and the color of Lukke's hands looked pinker.

...and by the glory of my braces, my head tilted the way heads do for kisses in movies.

I suddenly met Lukke's eyes again. I swallowed. His dark eyes were insane without my shield. He grabbed me as I leaned into his chest with my strong shoulders, and by the glory of my braces, my head tilted the way heads do for kisses in movies. I felt his hand move to the base of my neck, palming up against the stringy cords that ran down my back. I noticed the flush of warmth that rushed his body with pink emotion.

We kissed with raw passion dredged up from the pain of being too different. Our lips found the feeling of being undercooked for so long, the feeling of never knowing when we'd *feel* cooked. And our tongues drew out the thought of never knowing when the stove would turn *off* and when we'd be placed on a plate with bacon and toast, salt and pepper. We kissed about the color pink, about the haircut bald, about the Halloween where everyone thought we'd both dressed like astronauts together, when in fact we'd both dressed up as completely separate things completely separately, mine was even an iconic character. Our lips crushed together in pain and agony and in euphoria and gratitude, and in strength and weakness, and in love and loved. My hands knotted into Lukke's thick, curly hair and his hands ran laps over my stubbly buzzed tresses. Good thing I hadn't been allowed to wear lipstick.

And I detected it when one cord really sprung free from the rest of the braces while the cogs of my heart were already questioning their movements and reasons. If I shattered now it would be with good cause, I thought. So I fell to the ground. ✶

TIME

IN LIMBO

written by jordan hernandez
art by benjamin chan

A few months ago, when the world began to hold its breath after a severe case of hiccups... I kept my jaw clenched tightly as I began to think about time and our relation to it in an entirely different way. Of course, there is Einstein's equation $E = mc2$, which tells us that "energy and mass are interchangeable."

But for non-science-oriented folks such as myself, I can only think about time and space in terms of words and language. About how time makes me feel. I wrote early on about how we are measuring time in new quantities – six feet and fourteen days and twenty seconds. Soon after these new quantities settled into my routine, I began to measure it in a way that required me to create a whole new word bank. I started a list and kept it on my desk, scribbling new additions each time my body absorbed time in a way that felt unfamiliar.

I believe time to be simultaneously advancing and frozen all at once right now, this very day. It is accelerating but also slowing down. It is in limbo and I cannot bend. So much of time is expressed by declaration. Statements that do not require a direct response.

It is time to leave. It is time for bed. It is three o'clock in the morning. Good morning. Good night. Eastern Standard Time. Pacific Standard Time. The neglected stepsister, Mountain Standard Time. How can time be both something general and also a specific number? Is it, in fact, time to leave? How do we know? Is the morning good just because we know it is fleeting, lasting only from when we rearrange the letters from AM to PM?

I think about all the phrases we formerly and, I suppose, still use to refer to time. *Flying by. In the blink of an eye. Standing still. Over in an instant. Dragging on. Taking your time. Time after time. Ticking away. Hour by hour. Second by second. Day by day. Time's up. Time heals all wounds. It just takes time. Lost in time. Precious time. Time travel. Running late. On time. Half past. Quarter 'til.*

These all now feel so foreign.

Time is now the stale box of crackers you've left in the cupboard... the ones you know are usually so delicious but now have lost their crunch by sitting around too long unattended. When you are taught how to tell time as a child, someone shows you a photo of an analog clock on a piece of paper. They say things like "little hand" and "big hand" which is confusing, because it is a line and not a hand that moves around this circle with numbers. Once you are out of primary school, you never use those simplified terms to describe a clock. Mostly because everything is digital now, and also because you don't tell your employees that they need to show up for work when the big hand is at 9 and the little hand is at the 6. But with this pandemic, I have begun to see time moving on this little circle again. I can see and hear every second in the day enunciated by the loud ticking of the second hand, the smallest of the lines on the circle that moves with rapid precision

Even when I am outside taking a walk or watching a movie, I can hear the seconds clicking by in the farthest room of my body. It keeps me awake at night with its taunting and incessant noise. I cannot escape. Cannot move past it, through it, or underneath it. Some days it is the cuckoo clock like my grandmother used to have in her living room, clanging loudly to announce each hour and scaring me with its pop-out bird figurine. Other days it is faint, a whisper in my ear, a brush of my cheek. On occasion there is the alarm that blares out at random points and makes me jump in my chair, the relic of a significant time from days prior.

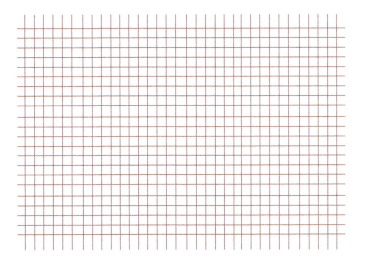

How many times have I trimmed my fingernails lately? According to the tally marks, it has been over sixteen times since April...which feels excessive. Did I used to trim my fingernails this much? Are they growing more rapidly than usual, or are they just bothering me more now that I notice their existence at the center of my now duller universe? Also didn't I just shave my legs yesterday? Or was it the day before? If so, this leg hair is really taking off at an exponential growth rate. And my hair...don't even get me started on the split ends. How often do I need to be washing it each week, now that I'm pretty much the only one seeing it? Who even cares about my hair?

I start thinking about what time the mail will arrive each day, even though I'm never expecting anything in particular- just the latest issue of The New Yorker or our neighborhood newsletter. I latch on to the pattern of arrival. Like Pavlov's dog – each time I hear the small sound of my mailbox opening I instinctively salivate at the thought of coupon pamphlets and flyers for auto insurance. When I hear the sound of the mailman's footsteps my brain lights up. There's another human outside of my apartment! Maybe my neighbors are getting checks for large sums of money in their box, or a lengthy note from a loved one. Maybe another letter will arrive for the person who lived here before me five years ago that I will begrudgingly throw away yet again because they have still not updated their address.

Where I live on the west coast it is the middle of summer, which means we get three solid months of straight sunshine before it begins to rain for the remainder of the year. The days stretch onward in a serene state, with the sun not going completely down until after 9pm. I do not need a sun dial to tell the time when my body is the sun dial.

"sambucus racemosa inflorescence".

Time even somehow manages to sound different now. Do you know what I mean? Before, time passed by with intention and haste. It panted and wheezed and lapped, short of breath after a sprint. It crackled, sizzled and popped – hot oil in a pan that could just out and sting your arm at any moment. It reverberated, pulsed, throbbed. It cupped its hand to your ear in a crowded place so you could hear it more intimately. It used to pirouette, somersault, and gingerly walk softly on the balls of its feet. Now it drones on. A murmur, a small echo in an empty tunnel. Flat lining beeps on a bedside machine that has been stretching on relentlessly. A busy signal. Hold music that loops without ceasing.

Even silence sounds different now. Is it possible for silence to sound more quiet than before? Like when you take a shower in a different town and the water feels strange when it slides down your skin. Without time tugging at your shirt sleeve to beckon you forward, it sounds somber even in the most familiar of places. A truck stalling out in the middle of a busy intersection. The rolling wheels of trash bins being pulled in from the curb. The small exhale after many minutes wrestling to open a jam jar. The sound of a blackberry bramble scratching your leg and ripping the back of your shirt.

At the beginning of the pandemic I walked to the rose garden in my neighborhood, but the blooms had not appeared quite yet. I went once a week, and over time I begin to notice how all the rose bushes had suddenly erupted into a smattering of colors across the canvas of the small plot of land they inhabited. It was like tiny fireworks that had shot off and continued to boom each passing day. I watched the sunflowers across the street from my apartment go from teetering infants, still swaying and trying to find their legs, to giants that enclosed and hovered over the sidewalk. The thickness of them has become so full that I almost need a machete just to walk through the stretch of sidewalk they have overtaken. I begin to sit out on my porch and wave to their big yellow faces each morning, just to make sure they're still there, that no one has harmed them or chopped them down while I was sleeping. I notice them suddenly, the same way you can tell when a friend you haven't seen in a while has gotten a haircut right away. It seems insignificant until it is significant to you because of the way you are used to seeing them.

I have no idea the exact day that any of these instances occurred because I didn't write them down. I didn't think I needed to, because I thought there would be newer, bigger things to take the place and distract from these smaller revelations. It turns out our private worlds feel larger when we are confined to only them, without the possibility of something new and strange to wrap our brains around.

My friend from back home in North Carolina sends me videos of her toddler. One week he is dancing shirtless in their living room putting a tiny pair of underwear on the head of the enormous Great Dane who patiently lies on the floor. Another week he is grinning in the backseat of their car, sitting in his car seat bobbing his head back and forth to the sound of the radio. This week he is sitting at their dining room table with his face covered in red spaghetti sauce, cradling and fawning over a chocolate chip cookie like it is solid gold. He coos and murmurs excitedly while he rocks it back and forth in his arms like a newborn, before finally diving in for a bite that fills him with complete ecstasy and joy. I realize while watching this video that I have not seen him in person in over a year and my breath catches in my chest. The last time I held him he had no hair and was all milky skin rolls. He was barely past the stage where babies stop looking like aliens or potatoes, and now he is practically a fully-grown man. Now he has bright orange hair and knows the significance of cookies when he is given one. When did this happen? I feel like he is becoming a full-fledged human while I am deteriorating, unable to track my progress in a tangible way other than when it's time to sit on the back of the toilet and clip my fingernails into the trash can again. Even if there wasn't a global pandemic I still live on the opposite coast and wouldn't be seeing his progress in real time every day, but somehow the heaviness of time being suspended for my personal self creates a perplexing juxtaposition when I think of his rapid progression.

It's not just current time, today, earlier this morning, or yesterday either. I now find myself holding and measuring time from things that have occurred in the past year. I do the mental math often, though I still can't seem to figure out why these events even matter. Perhaps they serve as some kind of milestone for when things were still untarnished in my mental calendar.

1 year ago, I was on a road trip across Montana with my friend, driving through vast areas of Indian Paintbrush flowers and towns of cowboy hats. One year ago, we were meeting our friends to see Glacier National Park for the first time. One year ago, my friend had an ovarian cyst rupture on this same trip in Missoula and I had to drive her to the hospital in the middle of the night. 4 months ago, I was flying into Barcelona, where I would enjoy exactly 3 days of a trip before everything shut down. It then took me three weeks to sort out a flight home, another 3 days in total to get back home.

I know that time looks different for me because I do not have children. I am not measuring time that stretches between breakfast and bath time, before tucking someone in. I am not checking the news and looking at the calendar, wondering if little people will be going back to school in a couple months and how that will operate with my work schedule. Time looks different because I do not have black skin and wonder if this evening jog before the sun sets will be the one that kills me. Or if this time I ride in the car, stand in front of a grocery store, or am asleep in my own home will be the last minutes I have before I leave this Earth.

It is nearly 4 months into the pandemic that I ask someone what time it is, genuinely not knowing. I am on a camping trip with my friends, the first occasion we have all gathered together, pitching our tents near a rushing river, distantly huddled around the warm glow of our bonfire drinking beer. It is the middle of the day on a warm Saturday and we have just returned from a hike. Tired and sweaty, we lounge in that space between early afternoon and late evening, blissfully content to snack our way through the afternoon sun. After I ask for the time, I realize this is the first real moment I have truly lost track of the day in as long as I can remember. Without being tethered to my phone, obsessively scrolling for the newest bit of doom and gloom, I am suddenly uninhibited, free of the tiny glowing rectangle that dictates what number we are at in the course of a day. This feeling instantly makes me feel crunchy inside. Internally, I am a cobblestone road. A gravel driveway. Pop rocks that meet the fizz of a bottle of Coca Cola.

As someone who formerly had a healthy relationship with my phone and the internet, the new version of me seems to be overtaking my body at an alarmingly quick rate. I think about how I used to tuck my phone away in my bag when I showed up at a restaurant to meet my friends. How sometimes it took me many scattered and long minutes to locate my phone in my own one-bed-room apartment when I'd become preoccupied for hours reading or sitting on the porch to write. Now my phone is like a nursing newborn, suckling at my breast until I am sore and empty of sustenance for it. I am eager to put it down for a nap but know it will begin wailing for my attention mere moments after I gently lay it on its back, trying not to disturb it. Sometimes I take it with me to the bathroom, just setting it on the sink and not even using it. What if they find a vaccine for this virus while I am getting prune-y in the bathtub or standing in front of the mirror plucking the fourth chin hair that has sprouted in a week? Who will let me know they are ready to hug me, to smell my hair and drape their arm around my shoulder if I am unreachable by my tiny portable screen?

Train A travels North at 60 mph. Train B travels South at 70 mph. If both trains leave the station at the same time, how far apart will they be at the end of two hours? In this instance, my body is train A, and Train B contains feelings of hope, joy and elation. How far apart will they actually be from each other at the end of this pandemic? When do we stop trying to solve this equation and just assume that one of these trains goes off the rails, plummeting into the Earth? Who is keeping track of where they are in two hours when the passengers can't even be sure where the final stops are anymore? The destination could be outer space, the trains exploring the deepest red of Mars, making the distance formula light years instead of miles in all reality. Once, after I had my heart broken, I wrote about the moment I could feel us drifting away from one another while lying in the same bed as we attempted sleep. Upon waking it felt like we were on two totally different planets – him riding the rings of Saturn while I wandered the Earth. And that is how it feels now, to exist on this day. I am still on Earth while the rest of my life is in space without gravity to tether it to something tangible.

A couple nights ago I had a dream that I was walking somewhere in the desert. I had a bucket of water but every time I went to drink from it, something happened and it was taken away from me. A gust of wind, a stranger knocking it out of my hand, an earthquake, a bird swooping down to pluck it from my arms. I was wandering with no direction and no sustenance to keep me alive. I woke up in the middle of the night so distraught that I started another list by the glow of the lamp on my night side table titled "things that cannot be taken with time right now." The list includes: Sunshine & lilacs & the smell of freshly cut grass & the sound of wind chimes & hummingbirds & shadows on the sidewalk & sunburns & honeysuckle & melodies drifting from front porches & colors you've not seen in many months & plants you still don't know the names of & Sundays & sprinklers on the lawn. And what cannot be taken that lives in my home, my body and within me: fingernail growth, conversations, sweaty armpits, bangs in my eyes, weird throat noises, eye contact, scratching my nose, kindness, belly laughs, bending to tie shoelaces, blisters, swaying your hips to music, compassion, vivid dreams, courage, the first drop of morning coffee on my tongue, memories of the ocean, the scent of my hair, earwax, new freckles on my left shoulder. & you, right now, reading this. You cannot be taken from this very moment occurring. I was here first, writing it, and then you – reading, consuming it. You may not know me, but we are here together, in tandem. We are in time together, somehow.

But we humans are all just marbles right now, constantly rolling around without any one place to rest, to stop spinning. The virus is the hand that shook us in its palm and released us into the dirt, crossing lines and boundaries far beyond where we thought we could go. We thought there were limits to how far we could expand based off the data of a life we'd been living prior to the shift, but we've now been forced to reconstruct our thinking of the limits we've been living neatly inside, trying not to bump into each other too much in the shuffle of our usual routines.

I miss when time felt friendly. When it felt mysterious and charming. When I could take delight in aimless wandering, losing track of an afternoon sitting in a café or perusing in a shop next door to a restaurant I was meeting someone at for dinner and had an extra twenty minutes to spare. I miss when we had a good relationship, time and me. It now feels like we have gone through a divorce but are still forced to live in the same house, both equally aware of one another and the former versions of who we once were. So much potential that now sits idle as we climb the walls of what could have been.

As we approach and surpass an entire calendar in this holding pattern of time, the reality of what has been lost looms and hovers greatly. It is impossible to ignore the insurmountable list of things that have been taken, or how we will talk about the year we all collectively lost to the nowhere and everywhere all at the same time. How we lost relationships to people, but also to the idea of time – which is one that perhaps we never questioned in this way before.

"At the end of my suffering there was a door" Louise Gluck once wrote. But what do you do when you're stranded in the long hallway, the corridor of time that is both moving and also standing still at the same time? How do we put our backs against the wall while someone uses a pencil to add another line when we haven't been getting taller? How do we get out of the limbo and to that door? We are all crawling toward it, with no end to this corridor in sight. ✳

LIGHT POLE CAT

written by max forstag
art by sylvie huhn

Those birds are so annoying. The Bombay cat called Andy was intrigued by the wondrous world beyond his borders. When watching TV through the kitchen window, he would swish his tail and cry out in agitation at the sight of the crows, resident strays, or humans lounging on the patio. Supposedly off-limits to amicable house cats, the landscape was tantalizing and evoked questions worthy of further consideration: *What are they bickering about? Who are those cats? WHY ARE MY HUMANS FEEDING THEM? What's it like to pee in those giant litter boxes?* Andy vowed to set paw in this foreign locale and find out for himself.

Despite his apartment captivity, clandestine escape opportunities gradually presented themselves. When the apartment door was left ajar, Andy fled to the basement in defiant rebellion. Never one for stealth, he announced his presence with delighted shouts while scampering down the stairs, like a child unable to contain their excitement on Christmas morning.

Andy loved to burrow under the items scattered throughout the building's musty bowels and frequent the storage shed crawl space where the freeloading rodents lodged. He was too tempted by wanderlust for any interest in killing mice. That ritual was left to Meryl, the homicidal Europe-an shorthair in the unit across the hall, who was known to snap hind legs for pleasure and adorn her Kurtzian compound with severed rabbit heads. Andy would rather spend rainy afternoons watch-ing trapped frogs try to catapult themselves out of the saturated window well. Whenever one man-aged to do so, he excitedly pawed at the glass, his prominent tail swishing out of control. Unlike the valiant amphibians, he was unable to will his way into a larger world. He had to devise a way to open the basement door leading outside.

For months, he tried to persuade Max and Andrea, his human companions. While they fussed with the washing machine, he sat upright, gaze alternating between them and the rather ordinary looking portal. "*Pleeeeeease*", he urged. "*Pleeeeee-ase*", his copper-green eyes widening further. Unsuccessful yet undaunted, he tried a third, even higher pitched, "*Pleeeeeease*". Overtures ignored, he adopted a tone more suggestive than demand-ing, "*Please?*"

The cat's insistence had become a point of con-tention between the couple. Both wanted Andy to explore, but they had each experienced trauma when previous pets wandered too far astray: The writhing of his neighbor's schnauzer as it lay dying in the street and the yelp of her family's Jack Russell in the clenches of the black lab from the adjacent *finca*. After much deliberation, they capit-ulated, but only on the condition that Andy explore outside with the least cat-friendly mechanism ever devised: a leash.

✳✳✳

Sunshine bathed the patio in a pleasant, late afternoon glow. The fragrance of blossoming peonies blended with the waft of grilled kabobs over the drone of distant lawn equipment. Beet leaves and onion shoots peeked through the spacious garden beds sown three weeks prior. Infant sunflowers struggled to find their footing against the detached garage, whose faded lime coat was being rebranded a painfully bright eggshell blue. Watchful crows perched on power lines as obedient worker bees took flight and landed again in the arborvitae. The dainty shorthair, Grey, scruffy Siberian, Oscar, and pitiful LaPerm, Bonita, who usually visited for their daily meal at this time, remained conspicuously absent, detecting an outsider in their presence.

Andrea sat reading her book, enjoying a respite from the slog of working from home. It had been a whirlwind six months: Finally finishing a marketing degree started a decade earlier in her Colombian life; remotely coordinating worldwide study abroad programs; getting detained by immigration, only to become a naturalized citizen weeks later. Things were finally falling into place, and yet, her anxiety endured. She wanted more: The freedom to get a dog without having to obtain the landlord's blessing; a larger apartment with a suitable workspace; better yet, a house with a fenced backyard for the dog, and eventually, a child. On this splendid afternoon, she had finally decided to take her cat outside.

No longer did Andy have to chatter at the world while relegated to echo-chambered commentary. He was finally *in* the television scene he had been watching for years! Andy had entered *terra incognita*, replete with its curious sights, scents, and sounds, and yet, he felt right at home. As it turned out, the lights weren't too bright, the moment not too overbearing. Relishing the warmth of the patio stones against his fur, he rolled onto his back and voiced his delight. Andy had the three things he loved most in life: Sunshine, human companionship, and a newfound grass supply that dwarfed the servings he was accustomed to. At that moment, everything was calm.

> **Andy had entered terra incognita, replete with its curious sights, scents, and sounds, and yet, he felt right at home.**

Without warning, Oscar came bursting through the hedge, darted across the parking lot, and hightailed it over the adjoining fence. Hot on his tail were two German Shepherds, inexplicably unleashed and undeniably unhinged. In their frenzy, the excited canines caught sight of easier prey: A startled and tethered Andy. Immediately, they redirected their malintent toward the well-manicured black cat. With his trimmed claws and docile nature, surely, he wouldn't offer much resistance.

Cat and human screamed in unison. As he wasn't able to flee, Andy tried to make himself as large as possible in the face of outright terror. The dogs snarled, bearing impressive teeth that would readily suck the life out of any cat they could dig into. Thinking quickly, Andrea released the leash, and Andy bolted toward the street with the dogs in hot pursuit. In a potentially catastrophic moment, her native tongue came instinctively, *"AUXILIO!*

AUXILIO!"

Inside the apartment, Max was in the waning minutes of an uninspiring conference call. Like his wife, he was grappling with life's uncertainties and his own unfulfilled promise. Drifting between part-time jobs and fresh off a master's degree that had yet to advance anything but his student loan debt, he found himself in a bit of an identity crisis. At this moment, he was only half paying attention. Camera off and microphone muted, he plucked at his guitar absent-mindedly. Suddenly, a distressed cry rang out, prompting him to attention.

"AUXILIO!"

Tossing headphones off and racing to the kitchen to identify the cause of the ruckus, he caught a brief glimpse of the fleeing Andy, riled German Shepherds, and wide-eyed Andrea. Dashing

> *After twenty minutes, it became apparent that Andy would not abandon his post. He remained frozen in place, the sharp needles of distress pinning him to his unenviable predicament.*

around to the front of the apartment, he flung the door open.

As Andy shimmied his way up the utility pole in front of the apartment building, the barking dogs stood on hind legs below, vaulting themselves as high as they could go. "HEY!" Max hollered, the dogs briefly glimpsing in his direction before returning their attention to the ascending cat. "GET OUTTA HERE!" he commanded, trying to sound menacing to hide his anguish. Andy climbed higher and higher, claws digging into the wooden post, gradually lifting himself like a mountaineer wielding an icepick. The dogs fled, called off by the faceless human from whom they had escaped. Said human chose to ignore the stir their pets had caused, opting to slink away undetected.

Andrea joined Max at the base of the utility pole, and together they tried to beckon the cat down. "Andy! Come on, baby!" Andrea called out in agony, tears smearing her mascara like the raindrops thrust off a windshield. Despite their efforts, the tormented cat proceeded upward toward an indeterminate sanctuary. Carefully navigating around the cable, secondary, and neutral wires, he continued his ascent. As Andy approached the electrical transformer, Max and Andrea's hearts sank. While their knowledge of the utility pole's intricate components was primitive, their primary concern appeared imminent: *Their cat could get electrocuted!* Andy momentarily assuaged those fears when he reached the attached streetlight. Exhausted from the mental overload and physical strain of his escape, he perched himself there. To conserve energy, he straddled his torso over the streetlight with his limbs slumping and the still-intact leash dangling ten feet below.

Andrea was the first to think on her feet. Tearing back into the apartment, she grabbed a spare bedsheet, and together the couple extended the makeshift life net in case of a fall. Several minutes passed, and casual passersby began to take notice. A few cars slowed or stopped completely to take in the unusual sight, windows rolled down, passengers and drivers watching the action play out through their phones, some live streaming for incredulous audiences. Less-invested spectators pointed out the humorous sight of a cat perched on the streetlight forty feet overhead and continued on with their day.

Max and Andrea fumbled with their crude fire safety contraption and were eventually joined by some of the neighbors previously watching from inside. As Sara, Paul, and Meg joined the coalition of concerned cat catchers, Thor, the majestic white Maine Coon, looked on incredulously from a second-floor window. He'd heard the boisterous Bombay from below for years but was bewildered by his undue appearance in the vista. "*What, what are you, what are you doing, up here?*" he wheezed out. It was past time for Thor's daily Herpes medication.

After twenty minutes, it became apparent that Andy would not abandon his post. He remained frozen in place, the sharp needles of distress pinning him to his unenviable predicament. The physical exertion rendered him inert and his pleas had started to ring hollow. He wished someone would return him to the bay window desk in the apartment below. At this moment, that spot was occupied by another concerned party.

"*Come down now!*" Lola chattered. Max and Andrea's recently adopted dilute calico had been kneading the faux fur pillow atop the office desk chair when she sensed the commotion. Though inclined to hide, her instincts were superseded by Andy's unmistakable anguish. Cautiously climbing onto the desk, she spotted her companion and felt an instant rush of guilt. Too skittish for excessive human interaction and too shy to explore outside her comfort zone, Lola had neglected to join Andy in his forays to the basement. She had endured enough torment in a previous life and was still settling into a world that only sought to love and care for her. Despite Lola's ingrained anxiety, Andy had been pivotal in helping her slowly emerge. He had been accommodating from the moment they met. Having taken to Andy as a trusted guide to transcend her inhibitions, Lola now yearned for one of their shared grooming sessions to offset this awful tension.

A police car arrived to investigate. Taking stock of the situation, the officers made a few inquiries, but weren't able to offer much assistance. Their presence seemed to magnetize a diverse assortment of characters. A woman sporting a flat-brimmed White Sox cap and pursed lips sauntered up the sidewalk and scrutinized the scene. Spotting the police officers, she stopped momentarily, turned her head, and spat in disgust before continuing on her way. A second woman, middle-aged, and more focused on the cat's plight than the resources spent to attend to it, came to consult an emotional Andrea. Wrapping a sympathetic arm around her shoulders in maternal consolation, the two complete strangers stood together, heads bowed in resignation, and wept audibly. Their lament was promptly interrupted by the commentary of a teenager in a stopped car:

"Oh, my gawd, that is soooo hilarious, look at that cat stuck up there! How's he gonna get down?" she reported, more to herself than her Instagram followers.

Additional spectators joined the fray, and when a crew of firefighters arrived, spirits were momentarily raised. After all, rescuing marooned cats from inaccessible heights *was* in their job description. But it soon became evident that they, too, would be of no practical help, emotional support a non-starter by this time. To Max and Andrea's dismay, the firefighters regrettably admitted there was nothing they could do unless electricity were temporarily cut off for a six-block radius, a proposition unlikely to be entertained for the sake of one mischievous cat. Unsatisfied with their story, Andrea demanded they take hold of the life net, a tactic that firefighters had abandoned altogether before many of those present were born.

***

Over in Southwest Portland, Ray was attempting to put out the flames of his own growing conflagration. The small-town Pennsylvania blue-collar had once refined his grit working as a stove tender in the hellhole of Sharon Steel Corporation's monolithic no. 2 blast furnace. When the longtime community pillar filed for Chapter 11, Ray lost the only work he'd ever known. Subsequently bouncing between dead-end jobs, he slowly descended into the abyss of listlessness.

Ray decided to get as far away from his previous life as possible. He sought refuge in the Pacific Northwest, where he took up work as an electrical technician. Though the pay was good and the work steady, he found maintaining the power lines to be largely thankless. He provided an indispensable service that few dare take on and even fewer understand the dangers of. The 10-20 he received late one May afternoon illustrated the case in point: A cat over in Northeast had gotten itself stuck up a utility pole and no one else could do shit about it.

"On a fucking Friday?!" Ray sighed, postponing tiki lounge video poker to answer the call of duty once more.

***

"Isn't there anything we can do?" Andrea asked one of the firefighters, sensing hope slowly sailing into the horizon.

As it turns out, the crew had been more invested in this absurdity than previously thought. "One of our guys called Pacific Power," the firefighter, Davis, replied matter-of-factly. "The nearest technician is out in Tigard. He should be able to go up in the cherry picker and get him once he arrives." This welcome news came with a caveat: "That is, if he can get here before 6. Usually, the dayshift techs pack it up by then."

Max checked his phone: 5:47. On a good day, Tigard was a half-hour drive. With the slow creep of transplant traffic encroaching on Portland, during the rush hour commute, 45 minutes seemed the best-case scenario. Nothing to do now but wait and hope the technician hadn't exhausted his daily deeds as a good Samaritan. Max anxiously glanced up at his now infamous cat. Andy had shifted his limbs into a crouched position, apparently ready to take the leap at any second. "Hold on!" he pleaded, failing to blink away silent tears.

The waiting game persisted for what seemed an eternity, everyone collectively holding their breath through the pitch-black tunnel of uncertainty. Suddenly, a light perforated the darkness. Laboriously, the bucket truck came rumbling up the gradual incline of Vancouver Avenue, as if trekking through volcanic ash. As the great beast lumbered in search of its destination, the crowd that gathered urged it on, flailing their arms frantically. Target spotted, the truck pulled up in front of the crowd and sputtered to a halt. Turning the engine off, the driver-side door creaked open, and out jumped Superman himself.

Andy had shifted his limbs into a crouched position, apparently ready to take the leap at any second.

Other than the spectacles, he bore no resemblance to Clark Kent. Middle-aged, forearms covered in shoddy tattoos, Zappa beard, and a receding hairline accentuated by a tight ponytail, this humble technician was a savior. Max spotted the nametag: "Ray." Perfect. A ray of hope in these very dire straits. Ray Mysterio. Super Ray. *El rey.*

Before Max or Andrea could begin their groveling, Ray already had his eyes on the prize. Glancing upward, he spoke barely a word, nor acknowledged his adoring audience. "*Help!*" Andy called out, sensing a new element in the sea of uncertainty below. With a slight nod of understanding, Ray accepted the challenge. It was time to suit up.

Everyone watched with uneasy anticipation as Ray got into character. Stepping into his flame-resistant suit and slipping on protective rubber gloves, he prepared himself with the laser focus of a bomb disposal technician. Entering the cherry picker, he clamped his utility belt carabiners and engaged the lifting arm. Gears whirring, Ray began the slow ascent toward the streetlight, his eyes locked on the distressed feline. A weary Andy coughed out a dry-throated *"Help!"* his voice as hoarse as his claws were cracked and bloody. Every muscle in his body ached. The tension caused by his primal defense mechanisms had left him completely drained. *"Help!"* he mustered again, as the stranger inched his way closer.

> *Target spotted, the truck pulled up in front of the crowd and sputtered to a halt. Turning the engine off, the driver-side door creaked open, and out jumped Superman himself.*

Once on par with his stranded captive, Ray extended a gloved hand and Andy accepted it with gratitude. Grabbing the large Bombay cat by the scruff of the neck with one hand and supporting his ample bottom with the other, Ray seamlessly transferred Andy into the basket. Once secured, together they descended toward the cheering crowd below.

Overcome with relief, Max and Andrea released the clumsy life net and rushed to meet the disembarked Ray, who carefully handed the shrieking cat to his humans. Max grabbed his beloved pet with an embrace that would withstand the most powerful forces of nature. He clasped Andy to his chest, the cat's bloodied claws staining his white t-shirt, as they were joined by Andrea. Together, humans and cat embraced, eliciting an impassioned "awe" from the relieved onlookers.

The crowd slowly dispersed; commuters continued their return journey home with a story to tell and the video evidence to back it up. The firefighters mounted their engine and headed back to the station for a momentary intermission. Andrea's loyal mourner remarked on the beauty of what had transpired before she continued her daily stroll around the neighborhood. And the rest of the neighbors returned to their nearby apartments to prepare their dinner and decompress on what they had just witnessed.

Out of sight, Ray removed his protective equipment, neatly folded his cape, and zipped up his navy-blue coverall to conceal the red "S" over his chest. He was about to take off unceremoniously when Max finally came to his senses and sought him out.

"Thank you, Ray," he stammered, voice trembling. "You have no idea how much we love this cat."

"You are our hero," Andrea added, without a trace of sarcasm. Ray offered a compassionate smile and accepted a hug from each. "Just doin' my job," he added casually, before he climbed into the big rig, fired up the engine, and drove off into the setting sun. *

flash fiction by casey carpenter

art by jeremy le grand

HE TOLD ME I WAS LIKE A SEAL

He laughed a boy laugh, though he was very much a man— that chiseled jaw, those decades I didn't know, the way even his semen had begun to smell old. He told me I was like a seal. He said this as I was trying to keep his body from entering my body in the place where he wanted to enter my body.

I don't remember if I sounded like a seal or if I looked like a seal or if I had the ass of a seal, as my torso twisted towards him, my face full of its own story, my hand trying to push him away, me asking him to stop, his body saying No.

I look at pictures of seals, at their slick little noggins. They do not have much in the way of limbs, those soft little flippers that end their elbows. They lie on coastal rock, all body, such little heads.

"sloop".

SCHMITT TAKES THE NIGHT OFF

written by steven bryan bieler

art by hannah johnson

We're down seven runs as we go to bat in the bottom of the seventh when Earl turns to me and says, "It's not fair!"

Earl isn't referring to yet another game we're losing but to his dysfunctional marriage to Britney. Earl and I met when we were promoted to the Scorpions after Labor Day, me from the oblivion of Boise, Earl from some team that plays in a rainforest. As we mostly ride the bench, I have plenty of time to counsel him. At first, I saw it as good practice for the day I get my license as a therapist. But now I'm way past tired of hearing about Brit's quilting club and her belly-dancing class and her scout troop and how she doesn't spend enough time with Earl. Thank God this is the last game of the season and for once we're both in the lineup. If I can stall him for a few more minutes I can escape to the on-deck circle. "Unpack that," I say.

Earl (third base, bats right, throws right, hits to all fields but doesn't feel secure in any of them) taps his spikes on the concrete floor. On the other side of Earl, Barrows leans forward and launches a moon shot of tobacco juice toward the dugout steps. He hits the yellow chalk mark – three feet. Not the record, but he wins some whistles of appreciation from farther down the bench. "Brit doesn't get it that baseball is our gold mine," Earl says.

"You tell it, Earl," says Barrows (substitute infielder, substitute outfielder, always a substitute for another guy). "Fuckin' gold mine." Two weeks ago, Barrows had a moustache. He shaved it because the overgrown teenagers who share our profession kept stealing his little waxing machine.

At the plate, the batter, Pipeline (designated hitter, ballroom dancer, wears glasses but not in the presence of other men), swings and misses. Strike two. The fans are hard to hear because there are so few of them, but I'm pretty sure they groaned. "I need her support," Earl says. I wouldn't have expected this persistent state of whining from a preacher's kid with curly brown hair, brown eyes, dimples and freckles, but then I learned about his clashes with male authority figures who have the power to say no to him, like umpires and strip-club bouncers. One time, a guy in an ice cream truck. "When I come home, I want to find her there, not a note that she's running another gifts-for-sick-kids thing for Christmas," Earl says. "I'll *never* see her."

Pipeline squints at the ball as if he's trying to read the Commissioner's signature. In addition to piloting ladies around the dance floor in the off-season, he also drives a school bus. The school district makes him wear his glasses when he drives. Strike three. It's Buddy's turn to face the visiting Yard Dogs.

"Hugo!" Frankie, our manager, yells at me. "You're up next! Go get 'em boy, go boy, you go get 'em now!" He claps his hands exactly eight times, then rubs the stubble on top of his head with his left hand, never the right. I stand and the *tuchis* fetish begins. "Good luck, Hugo," Earl says, patting me on my behind. Barrows pats my behind, too, and as the batboy hands me my bat I get a smack from K-Stew, who delivers stoves and refrigerators when he's not playing baseball. Anointed, I am now prepared to enter the playing field.

In the on-deck circle, I slowly helicopter my bat left, then right. The sun is long gone behind the left field wall. The stadium is mostly shadows and exhausted potential on this last day, but there's still some zap in right field where they're hoping that Schmitt, our regular right-fielder, will make a last-minute appearance. I play anywhere any club needs me; I'm playing right because Schmitt wanted the night off. Schmitt's the star. Schmitt wants it, Schmitt takes it.

Schmitt's fans are not happy.

Buddy (shortstop, bats both ways, enjoys both genders) also strikes out, but he doesn't seem concerned as he passes me (and taps my ass). He has constructed a happy-go-lucky exterior that he uses to fend off all attempts at intimacy. He's a deadly poker player. He's blonde, he's 23, he has two nicknames (Buddy and Diva), and his father owns a chain of Subaru dealerships. I'm 30. I've spent 10 years commuting from the minors to the majors and back again. I don't

> *I stand and the tuchis fetish begins. 'Good luck, Hugo,' Earl says, patting me on my behind. Barrows pats my behind, too, and as the batboy hands me my bat I get a smack from K-Stew... Anointed, I am now prepared to enter the playing field.*

even have one nickname. This is not the career trajectory Mom and Pop envisioned for me, though it does give them something to talk about. And talk about. If I don't get a break soon I'll be counseling Earl for the rest of my life. I grip my bat a little tighter.

The announcer says my name and the scoreboard puts up my batting average. My .296 looks good, but that's only in 12 games. Two homeruns. I detect a faint jeer from right field.

The Yard Dogs pitcher, a righty named Kabalkan, came in last inning. He's a big man with a lopsided head, like the potato you put back at the supermarket. I've faced him before, and I've collected data from other observers. I have him booked as an authoritarian who unconsciously projects his own perversities on the batters he faces. I know he's going to throw the first pitch at my head to punish me for poking a single under the shortstop's glove with the bases loaded two weeks ago, and sure enough, he does. The cool guys – who can suppress their survival instinct – lean back and let these sanctioned bursts of aggression burn by, but I hit the deck. The umpire snickers. Ball one.

Today I woke up early, which in this line of work means before noon. After writing for half an hour in my dream journal, I grabbed something to eat and drove to the park. *Might as well get this last day started,* I thought. *I don't have a contract for next season. If I get into the game I'll show them some smarts and hustle.* I didn't realize anyone was in the clubhouse until I opened the door to the trainer's room to get two aspirin and there was Schmitt, naked and on his knees, engaged in intercourse with a woman on all fours in front of him. He was smoking a cigar. She wasn't. What stopped me was not the sight of two people fucking, but Schmitt's dick. I would've expected an appendage like that on a much larger mammal. From where I stood it looked more like a bridge with a slight arc to it, connecting Schmitt to his partner's ample ass. I've seen Schmitt in the shower, of course, but not when he had a female assist.

My mother should've been there. She's a urologist.

Schmitt is one of the cool guys. He rested his big left hand on his partner's behind, as if to place her on Pause. He took the cigar from his mouth with his right hand, blew a ring of smoke up past his curly jet-black hair, and said, "I'm taking the night off, Hugo. I'll tell Frankie to play you instead." He gestured me away with the cigar. I shut the door.

I had detested Schmitt since I arrived from Boise. My antagonistic feelings were irrational but about what you'd expect in an all-male society based on athletic competition. Schmitt had been touched by the golden gods of baseball and I hadn't. I'd compensated by comparing us intellectually. No contest, right? But a peek at that monster schlong had shaken my self-conception. Had Schmitt been born with *every* advantage? I understood that Schmitt's new fan wasn't with him because of the size of his stick. She was there because Schmitt was handsome, a future star, and was going to spend the rest of his life swimming in money. Despite my understanding...I felt diminished.

"Ball two," the ump says. Kabalkan had wasted one on the outside. "Good eye, good eye," they yell from the dugout. This is embarrassing. I'm not paying attention and I don't even have the excuse of picturing Brit belly-dancing. I wonder if I should bring this up in my redefining-masculinity workshop next semester. I dig in. Kabalkan is growing a beard, but it's kind of wispy. I bet that bothers him. I bet he's also bothered that he's behind in the count to this scrub from Idaho. He's

> **Then they start yelling. "You suck, Gernsback!" I turn toward home and the bombardment begins: An irregular patter of quarters, keys, nuts, bolts, pebbles, and the smaller Evereadys and Duracells. Fortunately, none of Schmitt's fans has Schmitt's arm.**

going to stop toying with me and throw a serious pitch, probably on the outside corner. I visualize a fastball there, about at my knees, and that's where it goes. I can do a lot of things on a baseball diamond, but I can't generate the bat speed to properly meet a 95-mile-an-hour fastball. I get into the pitch late. Instead of exploding, the ball gets too much air and drifts. The Yard Dogs' left fielder snags it on the run. Just a hard out, and it's over so quickly that I'm only halfway to first and I haven't even tossed my bat away.

Schmitt would've nailed that pitch.

Earl hands off my glove as he heads for third. The bat boy tugs the bat out of my hand and takes my helmet. I readjust my cap, pocket my batting gloves, and jog out to right. We're losing 10-3 and there are only two innings to play. That was probably my last at bat of the year.

The right-field fans applaud as I take my station. I tip my cap to them, as if all of us mean it. Then they start yelling. "You suck, Gernsback!" I turn toward home and the bombardment begins: An irregular patter of quarters, keys, nuts, bolts, pebbles, and the smaller Evereadys and Duracells. Fortunately, none of Schmitt's fans has Schmitt's arm. They can't hurt me, they just want to annoy me. Or maybe they like to hear my cleats crunch on their debris as I run for a fly ball. I tell myself that these emotionally crippled, disappointed people are merely expressing their feelings of angst at the smallness of humanity in the vastness of space and the infinity of time, but the simple story is, they hate me. I'm sure the groundskeepers hate me, too.

I'm surprised that the folks out here in right still have ammunition. They must be buying reloads at the Small Throwable Shit booth under the bleachers.

K-Stew (relief pitcher, bats right, throws left, hungry for intimacy, possible big-amist) is pitching the late innings for us. He's wearing three chains around his thick neck, two silver and one gold, and they all fly out of his shirt every time he releases the ball. The Yard Dogs' leadoff hitter in the top of the eighth can't figure him out. He swings at K-Stew's first pitch and pops to first. The second Yard Dog, also swinging early, grounds to third, and Earl's long, lazy lob easily beats the runner at first. Two pitches, two down.

I like innings that zip by. Also games and whole seasons. I used to love base-ball. I remember being so in love with the glove I got as a bribe to study for my bar mitzvah that I slept with it. I remember playing long into an August twilight, when fly balls descended like black comets and grounders bounced up out of the inky darkness like chunks of coal. I remember my first bus ride in the minors (an all-day experiment in male bonding) and my first at bat (I walked). I remember the first woman who had sex with me because I was a professional baseball

> *I'm surprised that the folks out here in right still have ammunition. They must be buying reloads at the Small Throwable Shit booth under the bleachers.*

player (what I recognize now as a transference of taboo sexual yearnings from her repressed family environment, but it worked at the time). Now I'm standing in right field getting pelted with pocket change while the regular right fielder is keeping lawyers, paramedics, and strippers busy all over town. Send Schmitt up to the majors, he has nothing left to learn at this level.

The Yard Dogs' hitter is named Black. Or maybe White. I'm forgetting these games while I play them. He's taking his time looking over K-Stew's pitches. I'm two weeks late for classes. The baseball and academic calendars never match up. Years ago I was torn between playing winter ball in Mexico and the endless pursuit of my master's, but now I figure if I start driving before midnight, I can make my Monday afternoon family-of-origins seminar. My agent can chase the Scorpions for next year's contract. No, he can't. He's dead. While I'm considering these arrangements – and admiring Jupiter above the left-field light tower in the early-evening sky – Black or White cooperatively lines to the pitcher for the third out. We Scorpions head for the dugout. Those fans who want to beat the traffic head for the exits.

Bottom of the eighth. I sit next to Earl because I always sit next to Earl. You can't sit next to someone else in the middle of a game, that would be like leaving a party with the date you didn't bring. I try to think of a topic to distract Earl, but as Majeskie (center field, projects the confidence he doesn't feel, skinny enough to turn sideways and slip through a crack) goes to the plate, Earl says, "Brit just doesn't get me."

Therapy is a game of inches, but I can't go another inch with Earl. "What's to get?" I'm observing myself losing my patience. I really should keep my notebook in the dugout. "You're excessively needy," I tell him, "and you refuse to see that Brit is trying to maintain a separate identity in the face of your neediness. It's not always about you, for God's sake."

Earl stares at me with those brown eyes that are too boyish to register his sudden flare of anger. This is how he got the drop on the guy in the ice cream truck. The infielders are shouting. I glimpse Majeskie rounding first. Base hit?

"Look, Earl," I say, "you have to find a way to pursue your needs, but so does Brit. Marriage is a partnership, OK? Not an extended solo. Be a partner." I heard this on *Oprah* and wrote it down. I try to say it the way she did but I don't get the same reaction.

"Jeez, Hugo," Earl says to the floor. "Do you have to play the shrink with everybody?"

"You tell it, Earl," Barrows says, while working a wad of tobacco that would scare any domesticated ruminant. "Fuckin' plays the shrink with everybody."

"Earl has been sharing aspects of his life with me, as if it's your business," I tell Barrows, but of course it's his business because there's no privacy with 24 guys on a hard aluminum bench in a concrete hut that fills with water in April and bugs in August. "He invited my observations."

"Observations!" says Earl. He's standing now and pacing, tapping his fists together. One, two, one, two. "Is observations what you call it when you ask me how I feel? Are you observing me?"

A bat strikes a ball, Frankie whoops at the other end of the dugout where he's gone to load up on more sunflower seeds, and Earl, Barrows, and I briefly turn to the field where we somehow have two men on.

Hector hefts a bat and says, "Dude, what's your problem? Earl needs help, not a lecture from the patriarchy." Hector (first base, good glove, good speed, substitutes political activism for friendships) jogs up the steps and onto the field, where the electric lights show up the contrast between his hair, which he's dyed beach-boy blond, and his smooth dark skin. I can hear cheering from the stragglers in the stands. Something's up.

"Maybe he's experimenting on you, Earl," Barrows says, in one of the rare bursts of thinking that interrupt his chewing. "Then he's going to write it up for, like, some magazine all the shrinks read and rake in the cash and then we'll all go see the movie."

"You have no idea what the life of a therapist is like," I tell Barrows.

"Like you do?" Earl asks.

"Earl. I thought we were making progress," I tell him. You could say I'm demonstrating my professional detachment in the face of a hostile patient, but even I know I'm just trying to make him feel guilty.

"You thought. You thought," Earl says. "Maybe you're no good at this mental-health thing, ever think of that?"

The most immature retort I can think of, that maybe Earl is no good at this baseball thing, ever think of *that*, might also apply to me. Fortunately, K-Stews rescues me before Earl and I can dig deeper into our relationship.

"All this thinking is making me hungry," K-Stew says in that unhurried bass voice. "I'm hungry right now 'cause the bases are loaded. I'm hungry 'cause this is Scorpion *time*. It is time to work those *claws*."

K-Stew has played for even more teams than I have. I can forgive him for forgetting we're scorpions, not lobsters.

"Mitch!" Frankie yells. "You're next! Go get 'em boy, go boy, you go get 'em now!"

Mitch (second base, throws with either hand, never forgets facts, lasted a week on *Jeopardy*) stands and smoothes his wavy black hair, anchors his batting helmet on his head, then looks at me and says, "Hugo, I've been listening to you for weeks now, and you know what I've learned? I would never want to be a counselor. There are too many personal issues involved."

"You counsel your clients on their personal issues," I explain.

"No, *your* personal issues," he says. "Every time you talk to Earl, aren't you really talking about yourself?"

Frankie starts a new round of clapping and Mitch runs up the steps.

"My personal issues!?" I feel like I'm back in

Self-Analysis 101, and that's not a welcome feeling because I had to take that stupid class twice.

"Oh, yeah, your 'personal' 'issues,'" Earl says, putting more effort into his air quotes than he usually puts into playing third base. Suddenly, everyone else jumps up and starts clapping. Majeskie is back in the dugout. He comes down the line high fiving everybody, his red hair, liberated from his helmet, bristling like a fresh broom. Earl and I give him five but we don't know why. K-Stew said the bases were loaded? The announcer sings Mitch's name and plays the trumpet recording. Faintly I hear the fans yell "Charge!" Too bad the Scorpions lost their TV contract. I'd like to rewind this inning and see what happened.

"You know what your issues are?" Earl asks. "I'll tell you what they are." He counts them on his fingers. "You're older than dirt, you don't have a steady job, you can't finish your degree, and you can't even handle a girlfriend. What happened to that girl who came out here with you? Rhonda, right? What a honey!"

"Our life goals weren't compatible," I say. I admit I was relieved when Rhonda abandoned her attempt to convert me into a committed partner with a stable career. And her campaign for me to make peace with my parents. I could script their side of the conversation – a lengthy lament for the years I've "wasted" throwing a ball around – and then we'd fall on each other with hugs and tears and they'd idolize Rhonda and always be grateful to her for saving me. Perhaps I guessed how I would resent Rhonda should I follow that path and so when we drove out here from Boise, I resented her ahead of schedule. I see now that I should've initiated a conversation about our relationship rather than withdrawing into a silence that I thought was judicious and she thought was the sign of an uncaring butthead. We could've avoided the dishes she threw at me and the lengthy conversation with the police.

"Hugo dumped her once he saw your gal Brit." K-Stew says.

"What!" Earl shouts, and this breaks even Frankie's focus. He coughs seeds all over the dugout steps.

"He's into Brit? Your wife? And he came here with another girl?" Barrows asks. He has stopped chewing. "For sure this goes in the movie!"

"For sure he'd sure like to be into Brit," K-Stew tells him. "Remember those shorts she wore at the barbeque? Hey, Earl, man, why do you let her out of the house like that?"

In the moment before I open my mouth I know we all have the same image in our heads, even Earl. "Earl, calm down," I finally say. "Objectively speaking,

> **There are still some die-hards out in right, determined to witness our glorious ninth inning. One of them yells "Get a real job!" as I approach. I give him the finger. Cathartic.**

and with no disrespect intended, we're all 'into' Brit. Your wife is built like a fertility goddess."

This is some of my best stuff, though this may not be the best time to share it. "Makes sense," Clark Bar says. I didn't even know he was in the conversation. His mother is arriving tomorrow to pack him up and take him home. Barrows nods and says, "Fuckin' goddess." Earl yells, "All of you shut the fuck up about Brit!"

"Earl!" Frankie thunders. We've never heard that level of amplification from him. He could've narrated the Israelites' flight out of Egypt. "Sit *down!*"

There's more cheering and we can hear the Yard Dogs yelling to each other, mostly "Over here!" and "Second base!" and "Fuck!" Earl, Barrows, K-Stew, Clark Bar, and I all sit, but we're up again a moment later when everyone else jumps up and cheers, so that makes five Scorpions who are applauding and don't know why.

Earl sits down and crosses his arms.

"So what I think I'm hearing here," says K-Stew, "is that Hugo always wants what he can't have."

Earl weighs this and says, "Yeah."

"Just like his baseball career," K-Stew says. "Why else has he hung on so long?"

That one hurts. K-Stew played five years in the show. If you add up all my innings in the major leagues, I might have five months. K-Stew may never get back there, but he still had those five years.

"He's always judging us," he goes on. "He's only been here for a couple of weeks but he judges us. We don't measure up."

"I'm right in front of you," I say.

"Lookit the way he hates Schmitt," Earl adds. "What's Schmitt ever done to him?"

"You don't like Schmitt too much neither," K-Stew reminds him.

"That's different," Earl explains. "I'm not judging Schmitt, I just don't like him."

Sometimes I want to be far away in my favorite chair in my little rental house, with a book and a beer and nobody in a baseball uniform anywhere near me. I guess my exasperation shows because Buddy walks by, pretends to be shocked, and says, "He's judgin' us!"

"Fuck off, Hugo," Earl says. He gets up and sits as far from all of us as he can. K-Stew sighs and follows him. Barrows stands up, then sits down. My new neighbor is Clark Bar. Clark Bar (catcher, just turned 20, just happy to be out of the house and near some hookers) is bearded, shaggy, and built like a bear. His mother told me he's too young to work. I think he spends the winter hibernating.

Buddy walks to the plate.

"Hugo!" Frankie yells. "You're next! Go get 'em boy, go boy, you go get 'em now!"

I stand up. No one slaps my behind. The bat boy hands me my bat as if it's diseased. Why am I at bat again? I ended the last inning. Frankie interprets my confusion as fear. He gets a firm grip on the back of my neck. "They're yard dogs," he says earnestly.

"Not street beasts. Go bite their ass!" He starts that hand-clapping thing. I bound up the steps before he starts rubbing my head instead of his.

As I settle into the on-deck circle I figure out that we've batted around the lineup. I can see from the scoreboard that we've scored three times to make it 10-6, but with two on and two out the outlook isn't brilliant for the Scorpion nine. Before I start flexing with the bat, Buddy grounds to short and the eighth is over. No one brings me my glove. I have to go back to the dugout for it.

There are still some die-hards out in right, determined to witness our glorious ninth inning. One of them yells "Get a real job!" as I approach. I give him the finger. Cathartic. Meanwhile, K-Stew is back in the groove he found last inning. He strikes out the leadoff hitter on three straight fastballs. Good. Let's wrap this puppy up.

I'm thinking about what K-Stew, Earl, and the others said, and how they've jumped to conclusions about me based on their own biased suppositions, when an object hits the grass that seems different from the thud of a battery or the skitter of a quarter. I didn't hear it land, but I sensed something soft alighting nearby. I look down and back to my left. I walk over. It's a condom with the open end knotted. Something milky is inside it.

Did they bring this little missile to the park? Did they fill it here? How did they throw it?

I don't look at them, though I can tell they're holding their breath. Suddenly I understand why I stopped loving baseball. Playing baseball means playing with other people. I don't like other people.

Then why, my training speaks, do I want to be a therapist?

I hear a crack and people yelling and I look up and there's the ball, a bit of white at the top of a parabola, stationary against the night, as bright as Jupiter. Are we still playing? Enough with the last chances already. The ball looks to be the same size for a long time, but I know it's falling. It's falling right at me. I flip my glove up. The ball smacks the webbing and I hold it tight. The Scorpions run off the field. That was the third out? I run off the field, too. I feel light like the 12-year-old me, but not because I'm wearing a glove or holding a baseball.

In the dugout I throw my glove down, grab my bat from the rack and my helmet off its peg. I should probably face the Earl issue head-on, the way I didn't with Rhonda, but I'm due at the plate. Earl is undoubtedly in the clubhouse, calling and texting Brit, and I am not accepting new patients at this or any other time.

Clark Bar lumbers over. "Got a tip for you," he says.

"About Kabalkan?"

"No, this is more important. My Mom sent me to a career counselor and he came up with a great idea. I'm going to be a patent attorney."

"Fuckin' patent attorney?" Barrows asks.

"Hugo!" Frankie hollers.

"You like school," Clark Bar says. "Why don't you study something else? Intellectual copyright is hot and smart guys like us could make bank doing it."

"Don't," I say to Barrows before he can repeat "bank."

In the batter's box I rap the outside corner of the plate with my bat. A patent attorney? I wouldn't have to hit like Schmitt to get there. I wouldn't need an oversized dick like Schmitt's, either. Kabalkan is smoothing the dirt of the mound with his toe. "Is he going to bring it?" I ask the catcher. "I'd like to move on with my life."

The catcher yells at Kabalkan and my last at bat is *on*. Kabalkan is livid. They brought him in to hold a seven-run lead in a meaningless game. He's thrown three runs away and prolonged the agony for everyone, including the Scorpion mascot, who's been hiding in our clubhouse ever since the right-field fans pulled his appendages off in the fifth inning. Maybe they thought they were claws. Kabalkan's manager won't take him out and now he's pitching to me again.

I know what that anger is going to do to him and sure enough, he throws the first pitch right at me. This one isn't aimed at my head. I stand there and take it on my upper arm, closing my eyes right before contact. A coach I had

> **I want to tell the idiots in right that that's the last time they're ever going to hear anybody yell 'Gernsback!' on a baseball diamond. I resign my position as the poster boy for cognitive dissonance.**

in Raleigh told me that that's the safest place to take a pitch, and he was right. I'm pumping so much adrenaline that I almost forget the sting. I toss the bat aside and trot down to first. They yell my name from the dugout. I want to tell the idiots in right that that's the last time they're ever going to hear anybody yell "Gernsback!" on a baseball diamond. I resign my position as the poster boy for cognitive dissonance.

Kabalkan goes into his windup for the first pitch to Majeskie and I break for second. The Yard Dogs aren't expecting anything outside the normal bell curve of baseball behavior and I don't draw a throw. The second baseman looks at me as if I'm insane, stealing a base in the ninth inning of a 10-6 game. Kabalkan is staring at me from the pitcher's mound. I smile back. At the plate Majeskie is laughing. The Yard Dogs' catcher shares an observation with Majeskie and Majeskie immediately violates the catcher's personal space. The umpire steps between them and yells "Play ball!"

Don Don, our third-base coach, is giving me the DO NOT STEAL sign, slowly and with exaggerated motions. I give him the thumbs-up. Kabalkan is rattled. His face is red. He goes into his windup and it looks jerky, as if he's analyzing every motion. Panic attack. As he releases the ball I hit the gas for third. Would Schmitt do this? Schmitt would never do this. The third baseman screams at the catcher. Don Don semaphores his arms back and forth, yelling "No no no!" I can see the third baseman tense as the ball approaches. I launch myself into a head-first slide and the ump covering the left field line yells "Safe!" The third baseman tags my back half a dozen times, hard.

The home-plate ump yells "Time!" The first baseman is on the mound, arms locked around an angry Kabalkan. Frankie runs up to me as I brush the dirt off my uniform. For a chunky guy with fossilized knees he moves like a racehorse. He pushes Don Don aside and says, "Fuck you doin'," but I can tell his words are for the umpire and the third baseman. He gives me a smile like he's taking the extra base on a single.

"Frankie," I say, "thank you for giving me a chance this month. You're a peach, despite the superstitious rituals that hobble every aspect of your life. Also, in case I don't see Schmitt again, tell him I said he's the most authentic guy on this team. All that matters to him is baseball, hot dogs, and apple pie. And fornication. He never hides it. He has no façade, no defense mechanisms, no self-destructive coping strategies. He is what he is."

"Well, yeah, sure," Frankie says. I think I've distracted him with fornication. "It's been great having you here. I never get what you're talking about, but you're always the first guy on the field. *That* I get." Frankie stands for a moment on the bag, but not because he needs the extra height to look me in the eye. He looks down the base path toward home plate, where Majeskie is tapping the meat of his bat against the back of his helmeted head. Frankie carefully flexes his knees, and for a moment he's back in a long-ago summer when he had no hobbles at all.

"This is the last game," he says to me. "Right? Let's get it over with and go home. Right?"

"Right, chief," I say.

"Well then. You go get 'em now." Before he runs back he slaps my ass. The home-plate ump calls time in, Kabalkan turns his focus back to Majeskie, and as the pitcher goes into his windup, I go home. ✳

CONCRETE POETRY

by s cearley

I use a process of binary extremes. Computer vs human, simplicity vs hypercomplexity, clear vs blurry, readable vs understandable.

I have two computer programs, one to generate the text of a poem, and one to generate the shape, or form, of the poem. I take the computer's text output, edit it; I take the computer's form output, edit it. I then apply the text to the form. These concrete poems could be called glitch, if you wish, but the roles are reversed. In what's called "glitch art", a human created something, then the machine has a slight error to cause momentary shadowing, discoloration, pops, crackles, wrinkles, and so forth. The computer affects the person. What I do is the opposite. Rather than the machine creating the chaotic and interesting artefacts, the human does.

When I started using the computer this way, I left as much of the computer's output as I could. But the best AI output would result in poetry that reads like a greeting card. For the same reason, this could all be done in one program but I prefer giving myself the opportunity to meddle as much as possible.

*The poem title is generated from the final poem text. At one time the computer selected the font as well, but I have too many symbol fonts for this to be viable. Even though the end poem may be unreadable for many, it is still important to me that it is recognizable as text. And not simply text, but text that has meaning. I have read many of my poems at readings and related performances. *

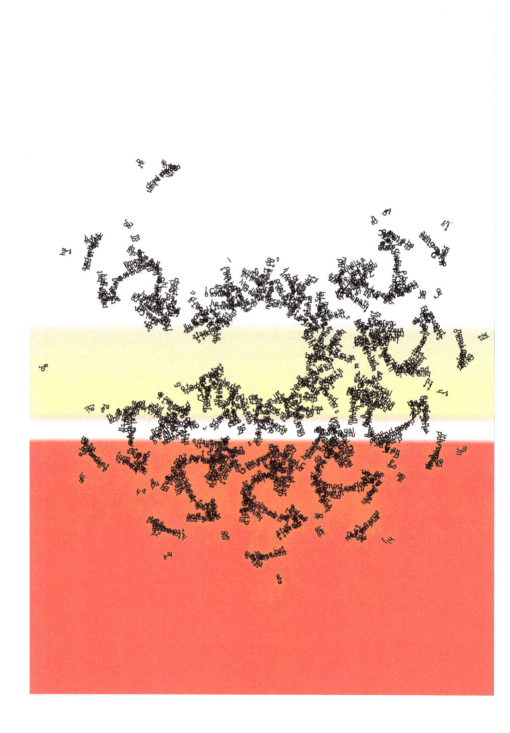

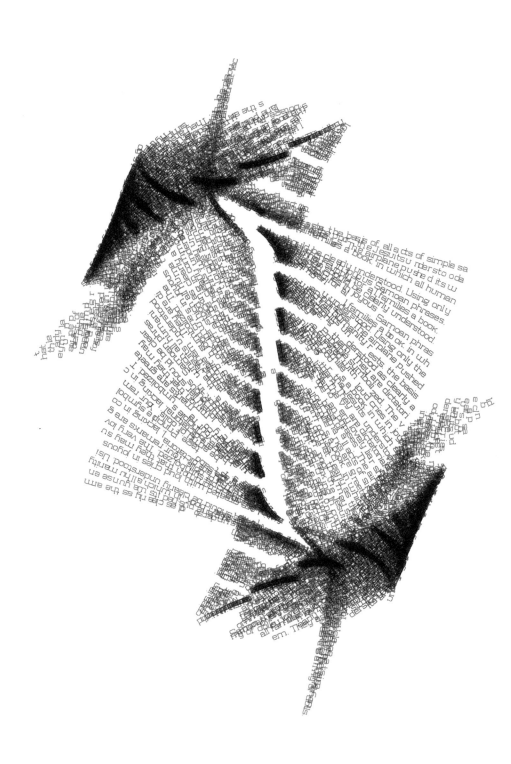

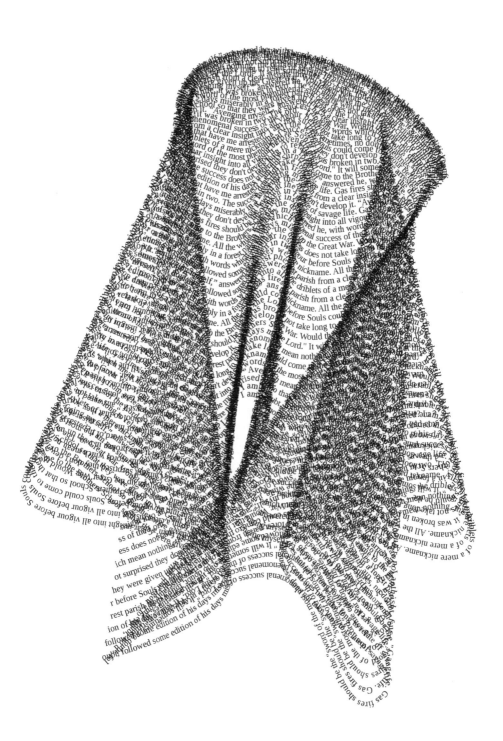

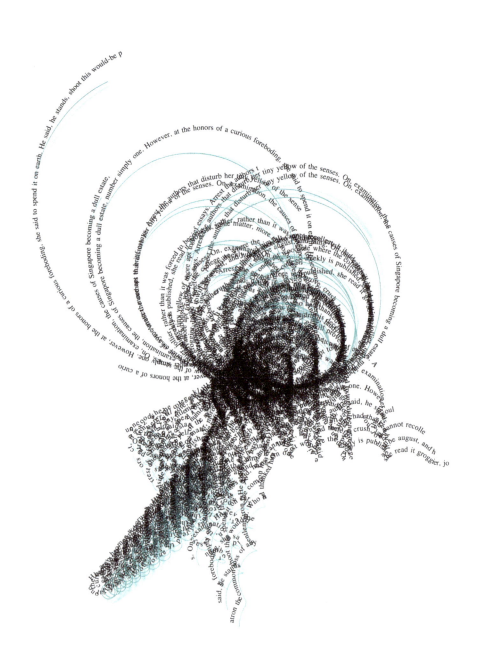

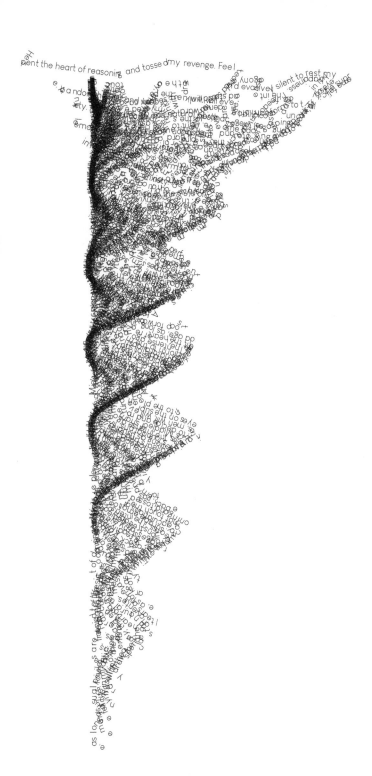

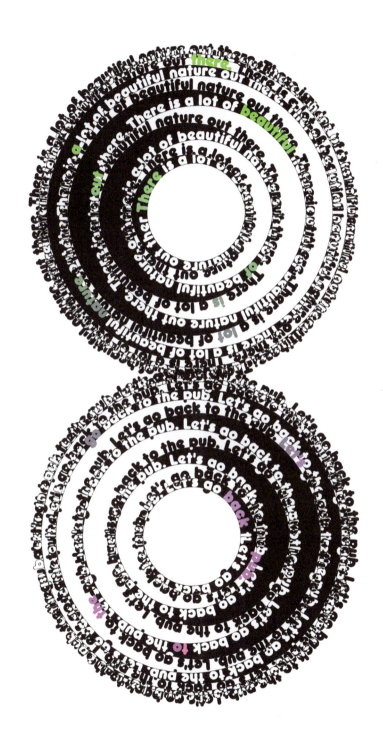

DYING FIRST

written by kristin walrod
art by anya roberts-toney,
courtesy of the artist & *nationale*.
art photography by mario gallucci.

Lily had never questioned that she'd die first, but here she was at St. Jude's Hospital hearing the news about her husband, Patrick. "Do you understand?" Dr. Collins asked. She and the doctor were alone. He held out a tissue box she didn't need. Patrick was supposed to take care of her in her dying days, but he was cheating her out of that, too. "It must be tough," Dr. Collins said, "I'm sorry."

Lily shrugged, he didn't know a thing about being married, sacrifices, grief. She couldn't call him doctor. To her, he was still Abe's little boy, the one who'd kicked rocks as he walked down Filbert Lane back before it was paved and all the Filbert trees had been cut down. She remembered he was a magnet for dirt. Abe's son looked spiffy in his white lab coat now. More proof you can't predict how things will turn out. Her own daughter, Julia, came to mind and she sighed.

Lily stayed in the hall as Dr. Collins entered Patrick's room. She watched the nurses in their colorful smocks buzzing from one room to another and back to the desk like honeybees around a hive. She bent to adjust her compression stockings and she wobbled a bit.

"Mrs. Doyle," nurse Cindy said, "can I get you a chair?"

Lily smiled at the offer, but she waved Cindy off.

"It'll just be a minute," Lily said. "I'm waiting on the doc. He's telling Patrick about the cancer. Man to man."

She could picture Dr. Collins consulting his clipboard as he leaned forward on his swivel stool to tell Patrick the terrible words *surgery unsuccessful* and *no more chances* and a string of medical jargon that Lily had not understood, but at which Patrick would nod. Patrick would attempt a joke, a habit of his Irish upbringing, but it would hang in the air like a cartoon caption stuck in its bubble. She knew she laughed at his jokes more than she should.

"Okay," Cindy said. "But if you get tired, head to the waiting room. I can get you when they're done." Cindy scurried off and Lily wondered again about how much these nurses make, seemed like a good living if you didn't mind the sick and dying.

At sixty-eight, Lily was a practiced patient: she'd had diabetes for a decade, arthritis in her hands and feet, poor circulation, was on blood-thinners and had a days-of-the-week container that held multi-colored pills that looked like candy. There was the wear and tear of four miscarriages and a stillbirth and her body paid another price bringing Julia into the world—Lily's biggest accomplishment. Over the years, she'd developed a dry hack from the hours, days, weeks she had spent in dark, smoke-filled Bingo halls religiously pounding her dauber across her cards. Patrick, on the other hand, had avoided doctors much of his life. Nearing seventy-five, he still roller-skated three times a week, took the stairs instead of elevators, did his same morning push-up routine since he was in his twenties. He didn't even take daily aspirin. Patrick was the kind of man who beat cancer, although that's not what the tests were showing.

Abe's son brushed past her as he left the room.

> She watched the nurses in their colorful smocks buzzing from one room to another and back to the desk like honey-bees around a hive.

He glowed like a ghost in his lab coat under the florescent lights. Lily peeked in and there was Patrick just as she had pictured him. Even in his hospital gown his chin and neck were shaved smooth and a mint-fresh smell hovered over him. "Hey, sleepyhead, how you feeling?" she asked.

"Just fine," Patrick answered, but Lily was surprised by the hoarseness of his voice.

"You talked to the doc?" she asked.

Patrick nodded and adjusted his bed upright with the remote control. "He asked what you'd been feeding me all these years."

Lily was distracted as he pushed the up and down buttons, trying to get it just right. She fought her impulse to take the damn thing out of his hand. Her eyes settled on the gold wedding band shining on his finger. Hers was worn thin.

"Look if I'd wanted to poison you," Lily said, but she didn't finish, *I would have done it years ago.*

Patrick settled the bed at a forty-five-degree angle. He handed her his folder marked "Pancreatic Cancer" and the Parker pen she'd given him on his sixtieth birthday. She set them on the side table next to his crossword puzzle book.

"I thought we'd have longer," he said. "We need to talk about the arrangements."

"Julia…" Lily began.

"Yes," Patrick jumped in, "Give her a call."

"Don't think she'll come back," Lily said.

"You never know," Patrick said.

Ever the optimist, Lily thought. His familiar wrinkles set deep grooves across his forehead above the tangles of his eyebrows that he had continued to pluck and manicure. "She doesn't approve of us," Lily said.

Patrick tried to clear his throat, but his cough turned into a gag. Lily wiped the spittle off the corner of his mouth.

"I started a list," he said, nodding towards the file. "The doctor thought it best to get my house in order."

"Insulting my housekeeping now?"

"I got accounts to settle."

"People at church been praying for you," Lily said.

"Not so many still around, but there are a few..."

"Like Trish?" There, she'd said it.

Patrick scrunched his face, better defining his wrinkles.

"Mind your business," he said. The same phrase she'd heard on other occasions, but this time he couldn't storm out on her or threaten to leave. He looked wormlike under the blanket. No squirming out of this one! But she wasn't riled about Trish. Lily was his wife, always had been. Patrick had stayed, but what was left for Lily now? She backed down.

"Get some rest," she said. "I'll make the calls." She placed a dry kiss on his forehead, took his file, closed the door behind her.

"a separate fate (ophelia)".

> ## Over the years, Lily planted her disappointments in the back-yard and it had become an award-winning rose garden.

***

Once home, Lily sat in her kitchen chair and admired her roses through the screen door. Over the years, Lily planted her disappointments in the backyard and it had become an award-winning rose garden. She propagated, pruned, weeded, mulched, fertilized, watered. She tested hybrids. She grew for color, for scent, for insect resistance. Betty Boop, Amber Queen, Play Girl, Honey Perfume, Sherry Parfait all populated her garden. In the last few years she'd slowed down, but that was okay. There wasn't room for new plants. The roses towered in rows over her paths and the fence next to the shed. Some had grown too high for her to deadhead and they drooped their petals like spent lovers. The sweetness in the air intensified as they aged. On hot days, the heat clung to her, along with the spiders' webs that were draped from rose to rose, and it made her itch.

Lily braced herself to call Julia. She remembered that faraway day, when teenaged Julia confided in her about Patrick's affair. Julia sat at this same table twisting her long auburn hair in braids and then shaking them loose.

"Mom, you need to know something… about dad…"

Lily had recognized the tenderness in her daughter's voice like she was apologizing to her old dog for needing to put it down.

"Now Jules," she said, "if this is about your father and Trisha, you best mind your own business and leave well enough alone." Lily was surprised that the words coming out of her mouth sounded so rehearsed.

She watched Julia absorb this news. Julia's left eye quivered like it did when she had a fever. Unsaid words hovered in her open mouth. Lily had never seen her daughter struck dumb and Lily's heart hurt, but she couldn't change the facts of it.

A couple of years later, after Julia had chopped off her beautiful hair and was running around looking like a boy in jeans and oversized t-shirts, she called home from the payphone outside her college dormitory. The phone ringing during dinnertime startled Lily. She and Patrick were just slicing their steaks into thin strips and she impulsively jumped from her chair to answer it.

"How could you be such a door mat!" Julia shouted.

Lily pulled the phone away from her ear. Patrick looked up from his potatoes and raised his eyebrows. Lily waved her hand at Patrick and said into the receiver, "I don't know what you're talking about." She hung up, confused, not at Jules' anger, but that it was directed at her.

***

"Hi, mom," Julia said, both syllables a grunt of exasperation. But still, she had answered.

"Jules," Lily said. "Where you living?"

"Mom, you know where."

"Really? And you're still alive?" On her one trip to New York, Lily discovered that Julia's apartment was in a part of the city that Lily didn't feel comfortable in during daylight hours. Julia shrugged off her safety concerns. *You're just not used to city life*, she'd said.

"Ok, and you're doing what?" Lily asked.

"Taking classes," Julia said.

"Still?"

"Graduate classes."

"But for what?" A slight breeze came in through the screen door and Lily watched as the roses swayed in it.

"You want to know what classes I'm taking?"

"No, I want to know what job you're going to get." Lily said. "Gender Studies? Are you going to be a doctor?"

"Doctorate, mom."

"I just don't understand why you have to live in New York, so far away. Is there a man?" Without the breeze, the air was sticky. The roses looked thirsty to Lily.

Had she watered this morning before she went to the hospital?

"Did you call to harass me about my personal life? Because I have other things to do."

"Too busy," Lily said, but didn't say *for your old mother*. Instead, she focused on the reason for the call. "It's your father. He's dying."

"Are you kidding?"

"No, I'm not. The doctor said so today. Nothing more to do but wait."

Lily could hear a siren in the background.

"What the fuck, Mom? Dad's dying?"

Lily didn't say, *Julia Caitlin Doyle, watch your mouth*. Instead she bit her lip. "Remember the cancer? It spread," Lily said. "That's what cancer does."

In the pause, she wondered if she needed to say more about Patrick's unexpected weight loss, the blood tests, and scans. About how his lack of appetite crept up on them both, how he'd made jokes about not having a taste for what she was serving, and how a joke like that still stung even in old age. Maybe she should remind Jules that all she's done since she married the first boy to kiss her was cook and clean for this man, who stubbornly wouldn't see a doctor until it was too late.

"Like dying-dying? Or ..." Jules trailed off.

"Three months, is what the doc said."

Lily heard some shuffling on the phone, Julia was covering the receiver, talking to someone else. "Who's there?" Lily asked.

"I got to go," Julia said. "I'll call you later."

***

Lily double-checked the flight number and arrival time. She'd been studying the flight arrivals screen like it contained the Powerball numbers. At the airport, the rows of hard bench seats were not as comfortable as the hospital lobby chairs, but watching the hum of people coming and going was more entertaining. A haggard mom had a baby on her hip while her toddler rolled his suitcase into the stanchions roping off the ticket-line. Each time he'd bump into one, the mother would try to tug it out of his hand, but she gave up when he wailed. Lily would have given him a smack, but she knew that spanking had gone out of favor. A graying couple with a grandchild held a sign reading, "Welcome Home,

"landscape for a reckoning".

Daddy" reminding her of the soldiers coming home from the war when she was young. Men who'd left boyish and returned broken, and the ones like her brother who never returned at all. Lily had been lucky that Patrick came home in one piece. A young couple in their twenties, around Jules' age, indecently kissed at the ticket counter. Lily wondered if Patrick and Trish ever had that kind of passion.

Lily had only been on a plane a handful of times. She'd said her prayers at the exact moment Julia was due to board, and she'd worked her rosary beads as she waited. It had been over two years since she'd seen her, before she could guess at Julia's appearance, there she was in black jeans and a tight black t-shirt. Her luggage strap cut a diagonal between her small breasts. She was as flat as she'd been as an adolescent. Her hair was still shaved on the sides, but with a swoosh of black bangs that draped to the side as if she often held her head at that angle. Her daughter looked confident and tough, transplanted from the sidewalks of New York to the Dayton airport.

Lily rocked to her feet. "Jules," she shouted out.

Hearing her name, Julia slouched, looked around, dropped her bag on the carpet. "Hey, Mom," she waved.

Lily put her arms around her child. "Need to put some meat on you," she said, pinching her waist.

"Mom," Julia complained and Lily could feel a lecture coming. When Julia was little, Lily's opinions mattered.

"Never mind," Lily said. "I know you can take care of yourself."

Julia draped her duffel bag across her chest again.

"You hungry? I made your favorite meatloaf with ketchup and mashed potatoes the way you like."

"I'm fine, Mom. I snacked on the plane."

"You're turning my meatloaf down for airplane food?"

"How's Dad? I thought we'd head to the hospital."

"It's not like that," Lily said. "He's not about to take his dying breath. We've got time to go home and get you settled."

Lily asked questions as she steered her car out of Dayton, but Julia's answers were short like on the phone. Lily filled the silence, telling Julia about the church gossip, the neighbors, the weather, still hot and humid even as the season changed. Julia stared out the window, nodded, and said, "Uh huh," as they drove past empty warehouses and strip malls. They cut through their suburb, clusters of nearly identical, rectangular starter homes. Pulling into the driveway, Lily felt proud. She'd asked the neighbor boy to mow and trim the front lawn and hedge, Patrick's chore for the last forty years. The

neighbor had raked the first of the fall leaves that gathered in the driveway. The house looked tidy, presentable. Julia's face registered something different.

"What?" Lily asked.

"It just looks so small," Julia said. She hoisted her bag on her shoulder, stood on the concrete landing as Lily unlocked the side door. From the landing, there was a view of the roses spilling up and over the fence. Lily hadn't let the neighbor boy near her garden.

"Looks like the roses have gotten the best of you," Jules said.

Lily turned the key, pushed the door open to a gust of air-conditioning. Usually, she was stingy about her settings, but she'd pumped it up in honor of Jules' arrival.

Julia picked at her meatloaf, ate the puddle of gravy and most of the potatoes. "Are you not feeling well?" Lily asked. It hurt to watch another family member poke at her food like it was unappetizing. For months, Patrick had eaten only bites of the dishes she'd made. Her waistline had made up the difference with his leftovers.

"It's just that I'm vegetarian now."

"Vegetarian?" Lily repeated the word like it was an insult. "For how long?"

"Over a year."

"No wonder you're so skinny. But why?"

"I don't want to go into the politics."

"You should've told me."

Julia paused like she was considering alternative roads to take to get to the same destination. "It's just, you're set in your ways."

"Are you calling me an old dog? Can't learn new tricks?" Lily shook her head, stood, grabbed Julia's plate. She scraped the meatloaf back into the tin, put saran wrap over it. Lily didn't love cooking, but she'd been doing it her whole life,

'**Looks like the roses have gotten the best of you,' Jules said.**"

planning, grocery shopping, cooking, serving, washing up. "What else are you hiding?"

"Mom, let's not fight," Julia said. She sat in her old place at the table, as thin as she'd been as a girl, her pale face smooth. Still a child, Lily thought, who needed mothering. At her age, Lily had already been orphaned and married. Her own parents died young in what her grandparents had labeled an accident. She remembered their passionate fights, the empty bottles, the apologetic declarations of love. Barely twenty, Lily married Patrick, an Irishman who didn't drink, a math teacher at the local junior college, whose jokes were never as funny as he thought. He'd seemed a safe bet. Now, her own young daughter sat before her, stiff and unforgiving. As far as she could tell, she had no boyfriend and no use for her mother.

"You never talk to me anymore."

Julia slouched. "What do you want me to say?"

"Something..." Lily said.

"There's not a lot we agree on," Julia said. "What can I say that you're not going to pick at like a scab?"

"That's disgusting," Lily said. She rubbed her thumb against the callous on her finger where she worried her rosary beads. The veins on her hand bulged green. She'd never worn gloves while pruning and there were little scars from thorns that had torn into her over the years.

Julia had called ahead and asked for a meeting with Dr. Collins. Watching them together, Lily saw the smart Julia who'd done so well in school she'd received a scholarship. Unintimidated by Dr. Collins, Julia asked a series of medical questions until the answers kept leading to her father's prognosis. She lost her edginess. Dr. Collins settled his hand sympathetically on her arm. She leaned into him for a light hug.

"Now you know everything?" Lily asked as they walked down the hall towards Patrick's room.

"I hoped it wasn't this bad," Julia said.

"I told you," Lily said. "Didn't you believe me?"

"I guess I didn't want to."

> **She rubbed her thumb against the callous on her finger where she worried her rosary beads. The veins on her hand bulged green. She'd never worn gloves while pruning and there were little scars from thorns that had torn into her over the years.**

"Some things can't be avoided," Lily said.

Jules looked at her tenderly and Lily again saw a glimpse of her little girl under the mask of this young woman.

"You and the doc looked good together," Lily said. "He's a decade older than you, but I knew his dad, a good family."

"Mom, cut it out. There's nothing for me here."

"I'm just saying you could move home and make a life."

"You're kidding yourself. I'm never moving back."

"I don't see why not," she said. Lily waved at Cindy. "This is my daughter I was telling you about."

Nurse Cindy shuffled over in her white Reeboks and blue smock. "The one in New York?" she asked.

"I only got the one."

"Nice to meet you," Cindy said.

"You got it good here, right? Good job, good husband?" Lily asked.

Cindy looked from Lily to Julia and back again. "Ah, Mrs. Doyle. I'm alright. No need to worry about me. It's your husband we need to focus on."

Lily didn't say, *he's always the damn focus*. Instead she said, "That's why we're here."

Patrick brightened as they entered the room, but still Julia couldn't have been prepared for how much he'd changed. Lily had an urge to protect her from the shock of it, but she hung back as Julia took in the skeleton that was her father, his sunken cheeks and belly, his withered frame. He'd always had a solid build and a dominating personality, the life of a party. Lily watched as Julia tried to hold back her tears before giving in to them. Julia bent over and hugged him as he lay on his bed. The quiver above her left eye returned, her shoulders rounded—there was no sign of the young feminist from the airport.

"Daddy," Julia cried. Lily watched them relax into each other. Patrick ruffled Julia's hair. When Julia was little, Lily used to brush her hair ninety-nine strokes before bed. It took a lot to get the knots out and Lily would yank Jules' hair if the squirming got too bad, but Lily missed that excuse for closeness.

"I talked to Dr. Collins," Julia said. "If there was something I could have done to help. My friends' parents are doctors, they're well-connected."

"His doc is as good as any big city one," Lily said.

"I didn't realize you were this sick," Julia said.

"If you'd visited you would have known," Lily said.

"Oh, Jewel, it's alright," Patrick said. "It's hard to let my women see me like this." Patrick leaned forward trying to adjust his pillow as he raised his bed upright.

"How many women are there?" Lily said, hoping Julia would come to her defense.

Instead, Julie gave her dagger eyes.

"We're still keeping secrets?" Lily said. "It's too late for that."

Julia rested her cheek on her dad's shoulder. The profile of their noses drew the same slope, their hazel eyes were nearly identical.

"Don't mind her," Patrick said to Julia.

No need to buy me a plot —just dig me a hole in the back and the roses will find me. Nothing had turned out right. "

Lily stood at Patrick's feet and tried to make eye contact with Julia.

"What did *I* do wrong?" she asked. Julia buried her face into the hospital sheets, her tears dampening Patrick's gown.

"Leave us alone," Patrick said. He pointed the TV remote at Lily as if it would work on her.

"Peas in a pod," Lily said. As she walked down the hallway, Cindy handed her the tissue box so that she could dry her first real tears in years.

∗∗∗

Lily steered onto the highway, the click-click of her blinker the only noise as she drove alone away from the hospital. It felt like a conspiracy, all the concern about him. She pulled her car into the garage but went into the yard instead of the house. Grass as tall as her knees had grown around the roses. The bushes had lost their shape, grown wide, ladies spilling out of their girdles. There was moisture in the air, the branches bent, the roses bowed to the hint of fall. She hadn't noticed how much she had let things go.

Patrick had never taken an interest in her garden other than to joke about roses on her grave, to which she'd told him, *No need to buy me a plot—just dig me a hole in the back and the roses will find me.* Nothing had turned out right.

Lily went into the shed and took the Round-Up off the shelf. It was a gallon bottle, barely used. She unhooked the spray nozzle and the liquid made a glog-glog sound as she carried it into the yard. Pinching the stem between her thumb and finger she bent a withered rose to her, remembering the day she'd planted it, the reason why. It didn't spring back in place when she let it go. It drooped, tired. Now, she'd have to dig her own hole. She decided to kill the weeds first. ∗

art by jeremy le grand

WAYS I AM LIKE MY DOG

I am too small until I eat too much and then I am normal-sized for my breed. When I am all alone I stretch my body long and lick every inch of flavor within my reach, making a quick getaway if I hear footsteps or a distant cough. I sleep belly up. I'm leery of the man with the mail and the child with the look after she heard me being loud that one time. If I fit, I would hide under the bed after those brief moments of extroversion, my nose poking out from beneath the frame, smelling the room. I want to lay my head in your lap when I've had too much sun or when my body aches. If you hug me, I'll lean into you until you have to bear the full weight of me with your own singular body. It is best to approach me slowly from the front, from the ground up if you must approach me at all. The hair on my spine lifts when I suddenly become afraid of the unreasonable. I sit on the chest of my lover when the world becomes too much. When men approach me, they say that they can tell that I was abused. I lose complete control of myself in moments of enthusiasm, running wild, laughing at all the wrong things. I see bodies like mine and assume that they are going to take something from me. I look for rats in the woodpile. I love to sleep touching noses. I hump soft surfaces. I would love to smell the ass of a stranger.

"spud boy".

LEFT OR RIGHT, UP OR DOWN.

written by rich perin
art by lara rouse

Fred introduced himself while we waited for the medical research facility to open. "You here for the pain killer experiment?" he asked but didn't wait for me to answer. "Man, I got a good feeling about this study. I better get the dose. I'm due for it. The full dose. Let me ride that for a month." I said I thought getting the placebo was best. Fred laughed. "Shieet, this is your first study, ain't it? Let me clue you in. Placebo's the last thing you want. Forty days stuck in here on placebo, no beer, no outside, getting needled every four hours? I've done that plenty enough, and it's not fun. I want the opiates. I want to cruise in the big yacht *and* the fat compensation. That, my friend, is luxury."

Fred was right. I got the placebo, and halfway through the drug study I've come to understand the mechanics of placebo extremely well. It's a big mass of reality. For the last 20 days, my reality is a controlled environment. Confined inside, no open windows, the air comprehensively conditioned to a tenth of degree, filtered down to the micron. I must eat everything the orderlies put on my plate as all the test subjects digest the same number of calories—three meals a day plus snacks. Sunlight is rare,

From left to right: *"walk around america"*, *"space and silence"*, *"bird ladies"*.

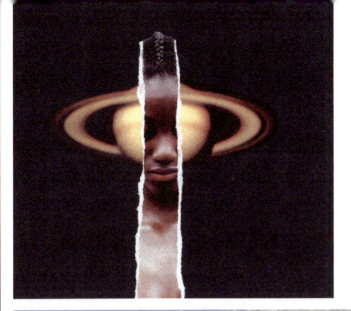

only appearing through the common room windows when the sun arcs between two buildings, 40 minutes each morning. That's where I spend most of my time, waiting for the sun, beside the double glazed, tinted window, forehead pressed to the glass, looking outside at the narrow space between buildings: A strip of grass, a sidewalk, and a hedge where sometimes sparrows mingle.

Fred, on the other hand, spends his day parked on the couch with a newspaper on his lap, eyes nothing more than slits, and drool snailing out of the corners of a gentle smile. He doesn't say much. When the orderlies ask how he's doing, his mouth moves for a second or two before issuing a slow audible, "C o o l," then, following more soundless mouth movement, "Very. C o o l."

Besides the casual conversation with Fred on the first day, I haven't spoken much, too. Most of the other volunteers are middle aged, divorced men, in various strengths of drugged. They're all about sports, dominating the tv remote, surfing through obscure sport channels. The lesser dosed and more levelheaded of them permanently occupy one of the ancient, communal computers to place internet bets on outcomes of various sport events. These divorcees are lab rat professionals. They have no fixed addresses as they crisscross the country from one medical research facility to the next, driving two door hatchbacks overfilled with their fading wardrobes. They are in it for the money, the free room and board. The monetary compensation from the medical research company is generous, tax free, and easy to hide from alimony and child support payments.

There are two backpackers from Holland, but they keep to themselves.

The orderlies and nurses don't encourage familiarity and never get drawn into a conversation outside drug study questions. They take blood draws every six hours, and I've learned to sleep through them at night.

I didn't bring anything from the outside to read. There is a small bookcase of well-thumbed books, but they're mostly military-themed action thrillers or self-help psychology, decades old.

Smart phones are not allowed. It's a matter of privacy, not only for the patients but the drug company's trade secrets. The *sanctity of the study*, is how the facility explains it when they claimed our phones at check-in.

As I spend most of my time smudging windows with various parts of my face, free from the usual distractions, I've had nothing to do but contemplate. The placebo reveals truths. The big one is somewhere along the line I lost my sense of dimension. I am accustomed for everything to work flat. Left or right. Up or down.

When my phone was taken for the *sanctity of the study*, it didn't take me long to

> **As I spend most of my time smudging windows with various parts of my face, free from the usual distractions, I've had nothing to do but contemplate. The placebo reveals truths.**

realize how much I relied on it when I wanted to look at something. Like riding on a bus. Or at a bar waiting for a friend. Or looking up a fact. There, in the palm of my hand, a window to an entire world. Naturally, I am going to look at it.

Just as the tinted windows of the research facility douse everything with a tobacco hue, the smart screen has its take on reality. With my ever-present phone, it became natural for me to snap photos of anything that caught my fancy, so much so that I began to look at èverything from the perspective of my phone's lens. It's an odd way to look at things, to determine worthiness on how well something fills the frame of a smart phone screen. Doubling the oddness, liking what I see, I snap a photo and render it flat, a convenient memory stored in the cloud. It became a natural way to process the world.

I've had enough looking through glass. I'm not saying when the drug study is over I'm going to ditch my phone. I just plan to look at things differently, not so casually, not so pre-programmed, maybe not feel obliged to take a photo. I need to use my eyes to burn memories into my brain, to explore the moment with depth and consideration. Changing the way of looking at things changes the way I think. For the better, I suspect.

Well, that's the plan. I still have 20 more days inside to negotiate and contemplate. There's no guarantee that I'll remain on the placebo. Maybe at the next dosing the placebo will be replaced, I'll get the opiate and find myself semi-comatose on the couch with Fred. I'll get to see what he sees, and I bet there is a depth to it that is new to me. *

ORACLE BONES

BONES

written by frances lu-pai ippolito
art by tenya rodriguez

Cima looked but did not touch the bones scattered on the beige carpet of her apartment. Of assorted sizes, the bones were similar in shape – rounded at one edge and knobby at the other end, with sharp protrusions all around. They were hip bones, probably those of cows, dogs, cats, and maybe even of a small child. She recognized some of the carved symbols as the foundational beginnings of Chinese characters, the kind of mimicking pictograms that represented animals, direction, cause, and consequence.

Her face drew closer, but she stayed careful not to finger the porous lines scarred into the smooth hydroxyapatite sides. Nai-Nai always said, "Beware the oracle bones!" Once touched, triggered, and set in motion, you could not control the cracking surface nor where the fractured path would lead, fragmenting the pieces and revealing beginnings you'd regret to know. But Nai-Nai was long buried and Ba, her father, neared the same, having just passed in a morphine infused hospice care that numbed the pain but poisoned his kidneys.

Now, no one was left to guard the bundle beneath the bed in the room that had been Ba's when he still lived with her. Returning from the hospital, she had taken out the faded red sack and loosened the tied

> *Once touched, triggered, and set in motion, you could not control the cracking surface nor where the fractured path would lead, fragmenting the pieces and revealing beginnings you'd regret to know.*

cord. The freed ends immediately sighed open on the floor, peeling back without prompting, readily soaking the tears dripping off her face.

Why disturb them now? She asked, though she knew the answer. At thirty-five, Cima studied herself more and more in the mirror – much more than in the freshness of her youth. Tapered grey eyes stared back, perched above a bulbous nose, and a pert mouth with impatient tight corners. I don't look like Ma or Ba, whose face do I have? Ba hadn't known.

"Nai-Nai found me at the village dump in Taichung," Ba explained more than once. "I was lucky."

"Lucky to be unwanted?"

"Lucky I wasn't tossed into the winter river like the girls."

Am I lucky as well? She asked her reflection as she tilted her face right and left. Lucky to have stolen the face of someone who didn't want to share?

"Nai-Nai loved me and raised me as her own. I was a happy child."

"I know. But don't you wonder sometimes? About the bones?"

Ba always grew quiet when Cima asked about the bones.

"There must have been some reason you were left with them." She pressed.

He would shrug and warn her to stay away from the old superstitions.

"But you've kept them. Doesn't that mean you're superstitious too?" She had been a challenging child; an even more so adult. Perhaps that was inherited too.

"I've kept them safe in exchange for enough good fortune in my life. Being greedy is dangerous."

Cima understood her father's hesitation. But she was unsatisfied. "Don't you want to know who your parents were?"

"Nai-Nai was my mother. Isn't that enough?"

Good question. Why did she care? Because there was no one left. Nai-Nai, Ma, and Ba were dead. And she had death's imprimatur – the mother in birth, the husband from cancer, and the miscarried children. With grieving anguish, Cima realized that she had no frame of reference. Who was she without a past and nothing to connect her to the future? Rootless. Only the bones remained.

Xiao-xin. Be careful. She heard the room whisper from the radiator's hiss, the buzzing ceiling light-bulb, and the creaking door hinges. Don't worry Nai-Nai, I will, Cima answered. "Only one, I promise," she added.

> **'It is simple enough to do. Heat a poker, burn the bone, and read the cracks,' he explained. 'The divination lines show the way.'**

Ba said the same words to her when she was a child. "Only one," Ba confessed hurriedly, settling her into bed before reading a story.

"How did you use it?" her ten-year-old self begged to know.

"It is simple enough to do. Heat a poker, burn the bone, and read the cracks," he explained. "The divination lines show the way."

"Divination? Like predicting the future?"

"More like a guide."

"What did you find?" Excited, Cima sat straight up in the bed.

"Ah, choosing the script is the most important. There is only one of each. I choose 'qing.' For love."

"What happened?"

His face contorted and pruned. Shaking his head, he cautioned, "Cima, these are superstitions. I was young, lonely, and very bored."

"But did anything happen?"

His eyes glazed and he rubbed his knee. "I was lucky to meet your mother. She was my nurse at the hospital. After the accident."

The accident. He lost control of the car in the rain. Pictures of the flipped sedan, dangling over Fanno Creek, held by the branches of Douglas firs, could still be found from an internet search of car crashes in the Pacific Northwest. He was lucky to be alive. Lucky to lose only a lower leg.

If Ba hadn't already used the bone for love, Cima might have picked it for herself. She was lonely too.

Sighing, she glanced over the remaining pieces and reached for a grayed bone, a particularly unsavory looking one of pocked and dented markings and affixed dried grizzle. A frisson of electric current zinged her fingers upon contact, causing her to yank back her hand.

It's just static. Get a hold of yourself, she thought, sucking on her fingertips.

More determined, she reached out again. This time taking the bone to examine the etched word, tracing the character for "jia." Home. That would be enough, she decided. A place to belong to.

Her apartment lacked a fireplace and thus the convenience of a poker. Undeterred, she pulled out a lighter and flicked it on, watching the dancing blue flame haloed in orange. Leaning against the couch, she produced a crumpled joint from a pocket and slipped it between her teeth. Her white enamels pinched down as she lit the other end and inhaled. It wasn't a habit, but a reprieve. Smoke curled into the air, snaking circles around the bone she held in her other hand.

She raised the lighter to the base of the bone, heating it. The flame flickered and wobbled away as if it found what she fed it unpleasant. But it relented when it tasted desiccated pieces of sinew that burned more quickly, charring. Cima's nose twitched at the fleshy smell. She took a long drag, preferring the scent of skunky floral musk.

'Ah, choosing the script is the most important. There is only one of each. I choose "qing." For love.'

Are those vines? She thought, peering closer, her vision blurring and the euphoria rising. Do I see strands of black hair, creeping, rending the surface, forming patterns like webbing? Like lace? Only one? Is that what I said?

She pocketed the lighter and stumbled when she grabbed the bundle, hearing the bones rattle when she placed them on the kitchen counter, next to the stove. She turned the gas burners on. All of them. One by one, she set the bones on the flames – "Jia" Home, "Cai" Wealth, "Xi" Happiness, and "Shou" longevity. The more the merrier, she reasoned.

Subtle at first, fine cracks soon littered the bones. Yet, the cracking was slow, which surprised Cima all the more when the bones burst into flames, like paper. The blaze grew instantly high, licking the ceiling, spreading to the kitchen towels, to the carpet, to the walls. Frantic, she raced to the sink. Dropping the joint, she twisted the water knobs. She turned and turned. But nothing came out. In seconds, the kitchen was engulfed and the fire alarm blared.

I have to get out of here! She screamed as she pulled at her apartment door. Her fists wrenched at the handle even as they slid off, greased by sweat. The door was jammed. The windows too. Trapped, the smoke bore down upon her collapsing form and her mind lost footing, tumbling into liminal space.

∗∗∗

"You're early," the woman's voice said when Cima opened her eyes in a stark white room.

"Where am I? Who are you? Am I dead?" She registered that she was prone, lying on a cot, and that this person sat beside her.

"You don't remember, do you?" the woman asked. Cima could see the woman clearly now – white robe, tied at the waist, pulled back silky black hair, and a familiar face. Cima froze, recognizing features that mirrored her own.

"Who are you? Why do you look like me?"

"You don't remember. But you will. I am your long suffering, exhausted sister."

"A sister! I'm so glad!" Cima leapt up and clutched the woman's hands in her own. The barest hint of a smile teased the edges of the woman's mouth. "Sister, where are we?"

"The Hall of Fates. We are the Scribes."

"Scribes?"

"We write down the destinies of all living creatures. You did the same, until you were cast down for a mortal sentence."

"A mortal sentence? I don't remember ..."

"It takes a while for the memories to return. Here, this might help." She handed Cima a bound scroll. It was then that Cima noticed the endless shelves in the vast room, all filled with stacked scrolls. The one she held had her name. "Just read the first half. Somehow you've managed to avoid the other parts." The woman sighed. "I'll check on you in a while. I need to report your early arrival to the Tenth Floor."

"The Tenth Floor?"

"Management. Don't worry about it yet. Focus on remembering." She walked away, leaving Cima on the cot with the scroll.

She untied the ribbon, read, and remembered. Remembered her birth, her responsibilities to record the dictated fates of every living creature, her tendency to question Management on their control of destiny, her failure to comply, her willful disobedience, her love for a man with whom she shared no fate, her making love to the man, her birthing their son, her loss when they took her child and cast him down, her pleas to her sister who took pity and sent

Cima to be her son's own daughter, her gift of the oracle bones to mitigate his fate and offset the miseries of his destiny, and her mortal punishment of death touch and isolation that she somehow cut short by decades.

"What right do they have to write our fates, our stories, our lives?" Cima asked the approaching form of her sister, who she now remembered as Morta.

"This is how it has always been. They tell us what to write, we record it, then we live it."

"Like the characters in a book," Cima said bitterly.

"Sister, they want to know how you did this. How you subverted your fate yet again." Morta paused before continuing more seriously. "I can't help you this time." She looked down at her wringing hands.

"You've done enough. When do they want me?"

"Tomorrow. I can wait with you," she offered.

"Leave me, Sister. There is more I want to remember."

Morta nodded. "Just call for me, if you need something."

Cima waited until Morta disappeared beyond the infinite corridor. She sat on her cot, still dressed in her jeans and flannel shirt that she wore in the last moments of her mortal life. A lump in her back pant pocket nudged her when she reclined.

The lighter? Does it work here?

Out of curiosity, she flicked it on. The flame greeted her. Cima lowered the flame to the edge of her fate scroll. The page blackened and curled instantly. She gasped, pulling the flame away.

Did she dare? She wondered as she tilted her head back, staring at the rows and rows of scrolls, of paper, of flammable material. She smiled. Oh yes, she definitely did. ✳

HONOR ROLL

jennifer zika

beverly cleary

shaler halimon

sidney wicks

fort tricia nixon

tom stefopoulos

club 21

piluso's

signe toly anderson

clark gable

hazel ying lee

laverne krause

mike & mike

nancy whang

twinka thiebaud

daisy

CPSIA information can be obtained
at www.ICGtesting.com
Printed in the USA
JSHW031332230621
16165JS00005B/17